About the author

Anneli Williams is an EAP teacher and cou... ...ctor at the University of Glasgow, where she has designed and taught English for Academic Purposes and study skills courses since 1995. She has authored two books in the Collins English for Exams Series: *Writing for IELTS* and *Vocabulary for IELTS*, and written numerous English language courses for learners in a variety of academic disciplines.

Acknowledgements

I would like to offer sincere thanks to my colleagues at the University of Glasgow, in particular Richard Davie, Carole MacDiarmid, Louis Harrison, Esther Daborn and Gayle Pringle for many years of collaboration and support. I am grateful to the team at HarperCollins, in particular my editors Sarah Curtis, Verity Cole and Lucy Hollingworth, and to my very patient family: Madeleine, Alice, Ruby and Steven. Finally, I would like to acknowledge my students, whose struggles and triumphs have taught me so much.

Contents

- distinguish fact from opinion
- reflect critically on your own views
- critically evaluate reading texts

- use a variety of note-making styles
- make concise notes
- organize and store notes for easy retrieval

- write outlines for different types of essay
- devise an effective argument
- structure introductions and conclusions

- learn how to integrate source material into your essay
- decide whether to quote, paraphrase or summarize
- learn how to quote correctly
- learn how to paraphrase and summarize

- recognize different referencing systems
- reference using an author-date system
- reference with footnotes
- know when a reference is and is not needed

- use sources correctly
- use sources effectively
- express your opinion in your essay

- get started with your first draft
- stay on topic
- use assessment criteria to redraft
- prepare the final draft

Introduction

Collins Academic Skills Series: Research will give you the skills you need for to select, read and use academic source material effectively.

Designed to be used on a self-study basis to support English for Academic Purposes or study skills courses, it is intended for students on pre-sessional or Foundation courses as well as for first year undergraduate students. It will also be useful for more experienced students who want to improve their library-based research skills.

The book has thirteen chapters covering the key stages of the research process from start to finish. You will learn how to:

- frame a research question
- find library and online resources
- choose appropriate source materials
- read efficiently and critically
- cite and reference correctly
- plan and write your essay

At the back of the book there is:

- a list of the prefixes, suffixes and root words common in academic English, and a checklist to help you read critically
- a glossary of key terms
- a comprehensive answer key

Chapter structure

Each chapter includes:

- Aims – These set out the skills covered in the chapter.
- A self-evaluation quiz – By doing this you are able identify what you already know on the subject of the chapter and what you need to learn.
- Information on academic expectations – These sections will help you understand university practices and expectations so you understand what is required.
- Guidelines on academic skills – These help you develop the skills to succeed at university.
- Practical exercises – These help you to develop the skills to succeed at university. You can check your answers and consult model essays at the back of the book.
- Tips – Key points are highlighted for easy reference and provide useful revision summaries for the busy student.
- Glossary – Difficult words are glossed in boxes next to where the text appears in the chapter. There is also a comprehensive glossary at the back of the book.
- Remember sections – This is a summary of key points for revision and easy reference.

Authentic academic reading texts

The book uses authentic examples of academic reading texts and essays in different academic subjects to help you apply what you learn to your own essay, whatever your subject.

Glossary boxes ⊆ POWERED BY COBUILD

Where we feel that a word or phrase is difficult to understand, we have glossed this word/phrase. All definitions provided in the glossary boxes have been taken from the *COBUILD Advanced Dictionary*. At the end of the book there is a full alphabetical list of the most difficult words from the book for your reference.

Using *Research*

You can either work through the chapters from Chapter 1 to Chapter 13 or you can choose the chapters and topics that are most useful to you. The Contents page will help in your selection.

Study tips

- Each chapter will take about five hours. Take regular breaks and do not try to study for too long. Thirty to sixty minutes is a sensible study period.
- Regular study is better than occasional intensive study.
- Read the chapter through first to get an overview without doing any exercises. This will help you see what you want to focus on.
- Try the exercises before checking the Answer key. Be an active learner.
- After doing the exercises in the book, try them again using your own research topic and reading materials. If possible, ask a more experienced researcher to give you feedback on your work.
- All university departments are different. Use the information in the book as a guide to investigating your own university department.
- Write questions you can ask to find out how your department expects you to do research.
- There is no one correct way of doing research. Use your experience of doing the exercises to learn what works best for you. Adapt the suggestions in this book to suit your learning style and context.
- Learning to do research is an on-going process, which means you need to practise the same skills many times. Revise regularly.

Other titles

Also available in the *Collins Academic Skills Series: Writing, Lectures, Numbers, Presenting,* and *Group Work*.

1 | Getting started

Aims ✓ understand the purpose of research ✓ learn about the research process
✓ learn how your research will be marked ✓ interpret set essay questions
✓ write an essay question of your own

Aims

Quiz
Self-evaluation

Read the statements, then circle the word which is true for you.

1	I understand why I need to do research as part of my course.	agree | disagree | not sure
2	I understand how my research will be marked.	agree | disagree | not sure
3	I know how to plan a research project.	agree | disagree | not sure
4	I can easily understand set essay questions.	agree | disagree | not sure
5	I know how to write a good essay question.	agree | disagree | not sure

What is research?

Glossary

subject discipline
In an academic setting, a subject discipline is a particular topic or specific area of study.

In simple terms, when you do research, you are looking for information in order to answer a question. In academic settings, research can take many different forms depending on the subject discipline and the kind of question you want to answer. If you are studying a scientific subject, your research may take the form of an experiment to answer a question which begins with the phrase: 'What will happen if … ?'. If you are studying a social science, your research may take the form of a survey of a group of people's thoughts, feelings or experiences. In any case, no matter what your subject discipline, at some point you will have to do some research which involves investigating what other scholars have said about the topic you are interested in. In other words, you will have to do some library based research.

Why do you have to do library based research?

When you do library based research, you usually have to work on your own. This gives you the opportunity to become a more independent learner and to show that you can think for yourself. These are qualities that are highly valued in academic settings within the English speaking world.

However, working independently does not mean that your research is not connected to the work of other people. One of the main purposes of universities is to produce knowledge, that is, to *create*, *evaluate* and *disseminate* new information and ideas. Producing knowledge usually involves many scholars working in different times and places. When you do research as part of your course, you are learning skills which will allow you to participate in that wider effort. You have the opportunity to develop the ability to:

- *Create* a research question and an argument to answer it.

- *Evaluate* the research that has been done by others.

- *Disseminate* your research by writing it up and submitting it for a mark, and, in some cases, by sharing what you have learned with other students on your course.

How do you know if your research is good?

In some parts of the world, students are judged according to how well they retain information given to them. In the English speaking world, when your essay paper is being marked, the marker will normally use other criteria for judging how well you have demonstrated the skills involved.

These are the questions the marker may ask themselves:

1   Has the student understood the question?

2   How well does the student know what other scholars have written about the topic?

3   How skilfully has the student evaluated the work of other scholars?

Glossary

synthesize
If you synthesize
different ideas,
you combine
these ideas.

4   To what extent has the student *synthesized* the information and ideas available to produce a convincing argument?

5   How clearly has that argument been conveyed?

6   Has the student learned what they were supposed to learn from the course?

Some of these criteria may be more important than others, depending on the task you have been set. However, in most cases, students who are good at 3 and 4 tend to receive higher marks. That is because they demonstrate good critical thinking skills.

Generally speaking critical thinking involves viewing issues from multiple perspectives and weighing up the strengths and weaknesses of arguments. When you do this you demonstrate that you can make fair judgements and take an independent stance.

For more information on critical thinking skills, see Chapter 7.

Tips   ✓   Find out what criteria will be used to mark your paper.
✓   Make sure you know what you need to do to get a higher mark.
✓   As you do your research, check that what you are doing meets the criteria.

The research process

Doing research is a complex process, so it can be helpful to divide it into tasks. How you break down the process depends on your assignment, your preferred ways of working, and your strengths and weaknesses as a researcher.

Remember, in practice, doing research can be a 'messy' process. You may do some tasks, such as making an outline plan, more than once. Or, you may do some tasks at the same time, for example, you will probably continue reading while writing your first draft. However, in general, if you are new to research, you should probably aim to spend about 50% of the time available preparing and gathering information, and 50% writing up. As you gain experience, you can adjust the length of time you spend on each stage. However, students who spend more time preparing tend to score higher marks.

Exercise 1

Imagine you have 30 days to write a 3,000 word essay on a topic related to your course. The tasks you might do are listed in the table below. Tick the tasks that you think are important. For each task you have ticked, write approximately how much time you think it would be reasonable to spend on that task.

Stage	Tasks	✓	Time
1 Preparation	Think about the research topic and the instructions given.		
	Find out what information is available – do some background reading.		
	Devise a rough outline plan.		
2 Gathering information	Gather books and articles from the library or online.		
	Read and take notes.		
3 Writing up	Write a more detailed plan.		
	Write a first draft.		
	Revise your first draft.		
	Write a second draft.		
	Proofread your second draft and make corrections.		

When your essay has been marked and returned, set aside time to carefully consider the feedback given. This will give you useful information about how to approach your next essay. If you do not understand the feedback given, it is important to seek clarification and advice. Although lecturers cannot always provide one-to-one meetings, your university is likely to have study advisors who can help.

Tips

✓ Think carefully about your essay question and why it is worth asking. This will help you choose a worthwhile focus for your paper.

✓ Do some initial background reading. If you discover that there is not enough information to support your chosen essay focus, you can choose another essay title.

✓ Write a rough outline plan before you start reading and taking notes. This will help you read efficiently and with a clear purpose.

Understanding the essay question

Sometimes set essay questions can be difficult to interpret. You may not know exactly what you are expected to do. However, if you break the question down into parts, you will find it easier to answer.

Essay questions can generally be divided into two parts:

1 The topic – this tells you the general area of your research.

2 The focus – this tells you what you need to find out about the topic.

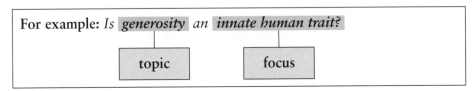

For example: *Is generosity an innate human trait?*

topic   focus

It is important to pay careful attention to the focus of the essay question because this indicates the boundaries of your research. The question *'Is generosity an innate human trait?'* limits your discussion to the issue of whether human beings are generous by nature. You should not be tempted to discuss at length other issues such as whether generosity is morally good or bad.

Notice also that the question requires you to focus on generosity in humans. You may find it useful to make comparisons, for example to behaviour in animals. However, you should keep your focus on human beings.

Once you understand the topic and focus, you need to think about how you are expected to approach the question, that is, what you need to do to answer it.

Exercise 2

Choose the option a, b or c which best describes how you should approach the question.

Is generosity an innate human trait?

a   You should answer 'yes, it is' or 'no, it isn't' and give your reasons.

b   You should evaluate the arguments for and against the notion that generosity is an innate human trait and come to a conclusion expressing your opinion.

c   You should write everything that you have been able to find out about generosity in human beings.

Instruction words in essay questions

Sometimes essay questions contain an instruction word or expression which indicates the approach you should take.

For example: *Critically evaluate media coverage of the 2008 banking crisis.*

instruction

In this case, you are instructed to make judgements about the media coverage. You might ask yourself: How good or bad was it? Or: To what extent was it fair, accurate, or thorough?

Notice how changing the instruction word changes the approach.

For example: *Analyse media coverage of the 2008 banking crisis.*

This question requires you to study media coverage in order to come to an understanding of why it was the way it was. This might involve looking for patterns or dividing it into categories in such a way that allows you to understand it more deeply. You might ask yourself questions such as: How frequently was the banking crisis mentioned in the news? Which aspects of the crisis were given most attention? What sort of language was used to describe the crisis?

Exercise 3

Instruction words often appear in the introductions to essays and reports. Complete the essay extracts below by underlining the most appropriate word in italics.

1   Section 1 will *discuss/justify* racial stereotyping with regard to the 'big five' personality traits. Section 2 *assesses/examines* the interplay between cultural stereotypes and media representations of minority ethnic communities.

2   This essay *compares and contrasts/outlines* the main components of the government's poverty reduction strategy… A final evaluation will *trace/assess* the extent to which government measures to reduce child poverty have met targets set in 2000.

3   This study will *trace/justify* the one-thousand-year history of the Catalan language. It will then *outline/compare and contrast* Spanish policy on minority language protection with that of the Scottish government in relation to Gaelic.

4   This essay will argue that there is little evidence to *justify/outline* arguments in favour of state intervention.

Exercise 4

Eight common instruction words and expressions along with examples are given in the table below. Match each expression with the correct definition a–h.

Instructions	Definitions
1 **Assess** the European Central Bank's response to the Eurozone financial crisis.	**a** Give a description or explanation of something
2 **Compare and contrast** social media use among young people in the United States and in China.	**b** Describe how something happened or developed
3 **Discuss** the principal factors that are commonly thought to influence a person's choice of life partner.	**c** Describe the similarities and differences between two or more things
4 **Examine** the impact of management style on teamwork in organizations.	**d** Give reasons and evidence in support of an opinion
5 **Give an account** of the role of ribonucleic acid in protein synthesis.	**e** Investigate closely and in detail
6 To what extent should parents be held responsible for criminal acts committed by their children? **Justify** your view.	**f** Make a judgement about something, for example how good or bad it is
7 **Outline** the key components of the United Nations International Strategy for Disaster Reduction.	**g** Consider a topic from different points of view in order to reach a decision about it
8 **Trace** the history of the comic book.	**h** Describe the main features of something

Exercise 5

Write definitions for the instruction words in bold below.

1 **Comment on** the key components of the United Nations International Strategy for Disaster Reduction.

2 **Illustrate** the impact of management style on teamwork in organizations.

3 **Relate** the principal factors that are commonly thought to influence a person's choice of life partner to Abraham Maslow's hierarchy of needs.

Describing versus presenting an argument

Some essay questions require you to describe, that is, to display knowledge without necessarily giving your opinion about it.

> **For example:** *Which regions of the world are most seriously affected by conflict over access to water resources?*

This question asks you to list and describe the parts of the world where there are the most serious conflicts over lack of water.

Other questions require you to present an argument, that is, to give your opinion backed by supporting evidence.

> **For example:** *How can conflicts over Nile River water resources best be resolved?*

To answer this question you need to give your opinion about the best way or ways to deal with conflicts over access to Nile River water. You need to give reasons for your opinion and supporting evidence, that is, examples and data to prove your point. You also need to show that other ways of dealing with the problem are or have been less effective.

Often essay questions ask you to both describe and argue.

> **For example:** *What have been the most notable conflicts over water resources over the last ten years and what are the most effective approaches to resolving these types of disputes?*

To answer this question you have to list and describe *and* present an argument based on your evaluation of the evidence. Be careful! It is often easier to describe than to evaluate. Less experienced students often focus too much on displaying information and not enough on developing an argument. Instruction words can also be categorized in terms of whether they require *mainly* description or *mainly* argument in the response.

Tip ✓ Remember that to achieve higher marks it is usually necessary to critically evaluate information and present a strong argument.

Exercise 6

Look again at the instruction words a–l below and answer questions 1–3.

| a assess | b compare | c contrast | d discuss | e examine | f give an account |
| g justify | h outline | i trace | j comment on | k illustrate | l relate |

1 Which require mainly description?

2 Which definitely require you to give your opinion?

3 Which instruction word is most common?

Note that the answers given in the answer key are suggestions only. In practice, you should interpret each assignment task in the context in which it has been set. Remember that certain instruction words, for example, 'compare and contrast', sometimes require a more descriptive response and sometimes a more evaluative response.

> **For example:** *Compare and contrast horizontal axis design wind turbines and vertical axis design wind turbines.*

This instruction requires a straightforward description of the similarities and differences between two types of wind turbine.

> **For example:** *Compare and contrast electricity generation from wind power versus electricity generation from hydropower in terms of efficiency, value for money and environmental impact.*

Here you have to describe the similarities and differences between two forms of electricity generation in order to make judgements about them.

Understanding long and complex essay assignments

Glossary

preamble
A preamble is an introduction that comes before something you say or write.

Sometimes essay assignments can be wordy and complex. However, these too can be broken down into parts:

1 The preamble: background information about the context of the question.

2 The question (or questions): what you need to find out.

For example:

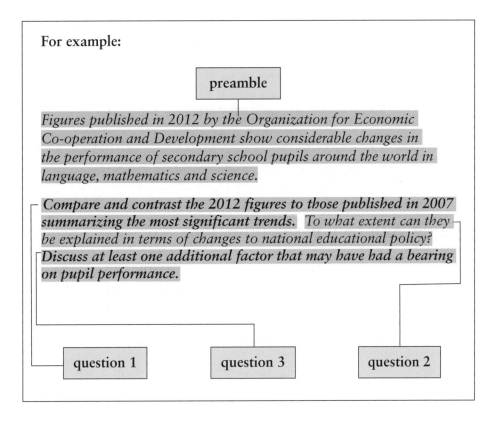

The preamble gives you important information about the topic and its limitations. Notice that you need to focus your discussion on secondary school pupils (not primary school pupils or university students) and their performance in three subjects: language, mathematics and science.

Note that there are several questions that need to be answered.

Question 1 requires you to *describe* similarities and differences and to *analyse* the two sets of figures in order to identify the most significant trends.

Question 2 requires you to *evaluate* the evidence that the trends you have identified were caused by changes to national educational policy. Here you need to present an argument.

Question 3 requires you to consider at least one other possible explanation for the trends you have identified. Here too you need to present an argument.

Writing your own essay question

Sometimes you may be asked to write you own essay question. This is more likely to be the case towards the end of your course when you have had some experience of writing research essays. To write an essay question you can follow steps which are similar to those involved in interpreting a set essay question. Select:

1 The topic: the general area you want to investigate.

2 The focus: what you want to find out about the topic.

3 The approach: how you are going to investigate it.

Choosing a topic

You will probably spend a lot of time and effort on your research, so it is important to pick a topic that interests you. However, your topic should also be relevant to your course. You need to use your essay assignment to demonstrate that you can think more deeply about an issue covered in your lectures and/or reading.

If you have difficulty identifying a suitable topic, try looking at your course outline and lecture notes. List the topics that are most interesting to you and that seemed important to your lecturers. Put your list away for a time. When you come back to it, see what grabs your attention most.

Narrowing the topic down

Once you have chosen a topic, you need to narrow it down until you have a focus. If you write about a topic without first identifying your focus, you will probably end up conveying a lot of information without examining it in any depth.

Before you start your research, you need to think about what aspect of the topic is most interesting to you. For example, if you want to write about the topic of *the internet,* you may decide to focus on: *the impact of the internet on how people relate to others.*

This is a good start, but the topic is still rather broad. One method for narrowing your topic further is to highlight the key words and list specific words under those categories:

> **For example:** *the impact of the internet on how people relate to others*
>
> Under *internet* you might list: online gaming, social networking, or access to information.
>
> Under *people*: children between six and ten, adolescents, young men from disadvantaged backgrounds, people who spend more than five hours per day online, etc.
>
> Under *relate to others*: form friendships, maintain face-to-face social networks, perceive authority figures, see themselves in relation to others, etc.

This method can generate more than one focus from which to choose:

> **For example:** *the impact of online social networking on how adolescents form friendships.*
>
> or: *the impact of online gaming on how children between six and ten see themselves in relation to others.*

However, make sure that you do not narrow your question down too much. If your focus is too narrow, you may not be able to find enough information to research it properly.

Exercise 7

Imagine that you are interested in researching *why some films become very successful*.

Narrow down the highlighted key words.

1 What type of films could you focus on?

2 What are the different ways you could define 'successful'?

Choosing an approach

Once you have identified your focus, you need to decide on your approach, that is, how you are going to investigate it. To do this, it is helpful to rewrite your focus as a question. Sometimes there are several possible questions. The type of question that you ask will determine your approach.

For example, you could write the phrase: *the impact of online social networking on how adolescents form friendships* as the question: *Does online social networking affect how adolescents form friendships?*

This question requires you to present an argument. You need to evaluate the evidence *for* the notion that online social networking has an effect as well as the evidence *against* and come to your own conclusion.

Alternatively, you could rewrite the question as: *How does online social networking affect the way adolescents form friendships?*

This question assumes that there is an effect. Your task is to analyse and explain that effect.

When deciding your approach, it is helpful to consider the context of your assignment. Discuss your title with people who are familiar with your course. Do some preliminary reading to find out what sorts of questions other scholars are asking about the topic.

You may also find it useful to break your focus down into several related questions:

> **For example:** *Does online gaming affect the way children see themselves in relation to others?*
>
> *If so, to what extent does online gaming affect …*
>
> *In what ways does online gaming affect …*

Exercise 8

Write an essay question of your own following steps 1–4 below.

1   Choose a general topic that interests you.

2   Identify your focus – write down what aspect of the topic interests you most.

3   Narrow down the topic by replacing very general words with more specific words.

4   Rewrite your focus as a question.

Remember

✓ Learn how your essay will be marked.

✓ When you receive your assignment, plan what you are going to do when.

✓ If you are new to research, aim to spend about 50% of your time gathering information and 50% writing.

✓ Prepare adequately by thinking carefully about your essay question.

✓ For set essay questions, notice the limits of the topic and identify the approach you need to take – make sure you know how much you need to describe and how much you need to argue.

✓ Divide long or complex essay questions into parts – analyse each part separately.

✓ To write your own essay question, identify a topic and a focus – make sure your focus is not too broad or too narrow.

✓ Decide how you are going to approach your research topic by rewriting it as a question.

2 | Accessing information

Aims ✓ find information in the library ✓ make the most of the library
 ✓ use databases ✓ make good use of the internet for research
 ✓ search effectively with key words

Aims

? Quiz
Self-evaluation

What do you think is the most useful way to find information for an essay? Rate the activities below from 1 = least useful to 4 = most useful.

1	Go to your university library.	
2	Surf the internet using a search engine such as Google™.	
3	Look through your course reading list and handouts.	
4	Use an academic database.	

Starting with what you already have

Before looking for information of your own, it is useful to think about what you already know about the topic. Make some notes of your ideas and any key information you have learned.

Then look at what information you already have about the topic from your course. Check your course reading list. If you have been told to read a 'prescribed' or 'recommended' book for your course, you may find it helpful to read or re-read any sections related to your essay topic. Check the references at the end for other articles or books that might be relevant to your topic. Highlight or make a list of the texts you want to find. Do the same for any photocopied course readings you have been given for your course. Finally, look through your lecture handouts and notes for any references to readings that are related to your topic. Add these to your list. Because these references have been recommended for your course, they are likely to be of good quality and suitably academic.

For more information on choosing suitably academic material, see Chapter 3.

Finding information in the library

You may be able to find some of the items on your list on the internet. However, you are more likely to find them in your library, either in paper or electronic form. When you have been set an essay topic, it is important that you go to the library as soon as possible as you will be competing for paper-based reading materials with other students on your course.

Most British and American university libraries are 'open-access', that is, users can access the shelves directly. Finding your way around the library can take a little time, so it is a good idea to get to know your library as quickly as you can. University libraries differ from place to place, however, most will work in a similar way.

Library catalogues

Glossary

intranet
An intranet is a network of computers, similar to the internet, within a particular company or organization.

The first step is to familiarize yourself with the library catalogue. A library catalogue is a list of all of the materials in the library. You can access the catalogue online in the library and sometimes outside the library through the internet and/or intranet. The library catalogue will list a wide variety of materials: books, e-books, journals, e-journals, newspapers, doctoral theses and so on. For most essays assignments, you will need to access books and journal articles.

Before searching for the items on your list, make sure you know what sort of texts you are looking for. In reading lists and bibliographies, books will normally be listed under the author's name and will usually include the date of publication, the title, the place of publication and the name of the publisher.

For example:

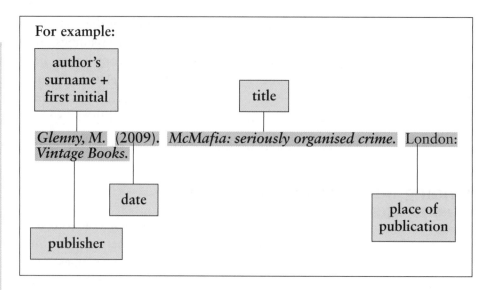

A chapter or article within a book will normally be listed under the name of the writer of the chapter and will include the title of chapter as well as the name of the editor of the book and the title of the book, the place of publication and so on.

An article in a journal will normally be listed under the name of the author of the article and will usually include the title of the article, the name of the journal, the volume number, the issue number, and the page numbers of the article.

For example:

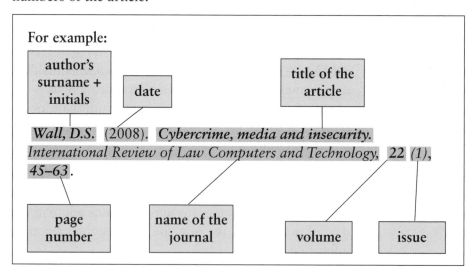

An online article will also normally be listed under the author's name and will include the URL of the item as well as a date for when it was accessed.

Exercise 1

Imagine you have items 1–4 on your reading list. Match each item with the type of text a–d.

1 Bialystok, E. (2009). Bilingualism: The good, the bad, and the indifferent. *Bilingualism: Language and Cognition, 12(1)*, 3–11.	**a** a book
2 Grosjean, F. (1982). *Life with two languages. An introduction to bilingualism.* Cambridge, MA: Harvard University Press.	**b** a chapter within a book
3 Simonton, D. K. (2008). Bilingualism and creativity. In J. Altarriba & R. R. Heredia (eds.), *An introduction to bilingualism: Principles and processes* (pp. 147–166). Mahwah, NJ: Lawrence Erlbaum.	**c** a journal article
4 Tucker, G. R. (1999). A Global Perspective on Bilingualism and Bilingual Education. Center for Applied Linguistics. Retrieved August 10, 2012 from http://www.cal.org/resources/digest/digestglobal.html.	**d** an article from the internet

Searching for books by title and author

Glossary

recall
If a library recalls a book, it asks the person who has borrowed it to return it.

You can normally search the library catalogue for books by title, author or key words. If you know the item that you are looking for, it is easiest to use the author, or even better, the title. If you are looking for a chapter within a book, make sure that you type in the title of the book, not the title of the chapter. For example, for item 3 in Exercise 1, type *An introduction to bilingualism: Principles and processes* into the search box.

The catalogue will show you whether the book is available and where you can find it. Sometimes several books with the same title will be listed. This may be because several editions of the book are available or because the library holds both a print and electronic version of the book. For print books, select the book you want and make a note of the location and any identification code given to the book by the library. This might be referred to as a 'call number', 'shelf-mark' or similar term. This code will give you information about the section of the library where the book is located.

If the catalogue indicates that the book is 'on loan' you may be able to recall it, either electronically or by requesting this service at your library help desk.

Searching for journals by title

If you are looking for a journal article and you know the name of the journal, you need to search using the title of the journal, not the title of the article. For example, for item 1 in Exercise 1, you should type *Bilingualism: Language and Cognition* into the search box. Journals are listed in the catalogue chronologically (with the most recent appearing at the top of the list), so it is important to know when the issue that you are looking for was published. Like books, journals may also be available in both print and electronic forms. To find the print version of a journal, note the location information. The most recent issues of print journals are normally shelved separately from older issues. Older issues of a journal are often collected together in 'volumes'. Like books, these are labelled with a call number or shelf-mark so that you can retrieve them easily.

Exercise 2

Imagine you wanted to search your university library catalogue for the items below. For each item, indicate the type of publication and the words you would use to search.

1   Small, G., & Vorgan, G. (2008). *iBrain: surviving the technological alteration of the modern mind.* New York: Collins Living.

2   Semanza, J. C. (2003). The Intersection of Urban Planning, Art, and Public Health: The Sunnyside Piazza. *American Journal of Public Health, 93(9),* 1439–1441.

3   Inceoglu, I., Segers, J., & Bartram, D. (2012). Age-related differences in work motivation. *Journal of Occupational & Organizational Psychology, 85(2),* 300–329.

4   Chan, K. W., Kwong, C. K., & Dillon, T. S. (2012). *Computational intelligence techniques for new product design.* New York: Springer.

	Type of publication	Search terms
1		
2		
3		
4		

Searching the library catalogue by key words

If you do not know the exact title of a book or journal, or if you want to find out what books and journals are available on your research topic, you can try a key word search. Start by highlighting the most important words or phrases in your essay question. Do not include instruction words or small words such as 'the', 'and', and 'in'. For example, if you have been given the question below, you could type in the word *management*.

Examine the impact of management *style on* teamwork *in* organizations.

The catalogue will show all the items that contain *management* in the title. If you get too many hits, narrow down your search by adding another key word, *teamwork* or *organizations* for example.

Exercise 3

Underline the key words and phrases in the essay questions below.

1 Assess the European Central Bank's response to the Eurozone financial crisis.

2 Compare and contrast social media use among young people in the United States and in China.

3 Give an account of the role of ribonucleic acid in protein synthesis.

4 Trace the history of the comic book.

Exercise 4

Type one of the key words or phrases you have underlined for each question into the key word search facility in your library catalogue and see what happens. Try a different key word or combination of words and compare your results.

Tips   If you do not get any hits, or too few hits using key words from your essay title:

✓ try using synonyms (= words that have a very similar meaning) or related words. Instead of *management*, for example, type *leadership*.

✓ or use a more general term. For example, for *Give an account of the role of ribonucleic acid in protein synthesis*, you could use *cell biology* as your key words.

Tips

Exercise 5

Write synonyms for expressions 1–4.

1 financial crisis

2 social media

3 young people

4 comic book

Try a key word search of your library catalogue using these synonyms and compare your results with your results from Exercise 4.

Accessing e-books and e-journals

To access an e-book or e-journal, you normally select the item, which then takes you to the provider's website. Each provider has its own website so they all look and work differently. In many cases, because the library pays for access to electronic resources, you may be directed to a login box where you have to type in your student identification number and password. This might be referred to as 'Shibboleth', 'Institutional login' or a similar term.

Glossary

copyright
If someone has copyright on a piece of writing or music, it is illegal to reproduce or perform it without their permission.

Individual e-journal articles can be read online, downloaded onto a memory stick or printed. E-books are subject to copyright regulations, which means that you can only download or print one chapter or section, or five per cent of the total number of pages. If you are not sure how much of an item you can copy, check with your librarian or look for relevant notices – these are usually displayed near photocopiers. You can, however, read as much of the book online as you wish. Many e-books providers also allow you to make notes and highlight text, which you can save and view when you next access the book.

Borrowing print books and journals

Different libraries have different lending policies. Books can generally be borrowed for several weeks. In many cases you may be able to 'renew' an item, that is, borrow it for an extended period of time if no other user has requested it. It may also be possible to 'reserve' an item, in other words, to ask that an item be kept for you when it is returned by another user. Some libraries may contain a 'short loan' collection, that is, a selection of books that are in high-demand. These books may be available for borrowing for only a few days or hours at a time. Reference books, such as dictionaries, cannot normally be borrowed.

If your library does not stock an item that you wish to borrow, you may be able to ask your library to borrow the item from another library. This is called an 'inter-library loan'.

The most recent issues of journals are not normally available for borrowing. You may read them in the library or photocopy one article within an issue. Note that there is usually a small charge for photocopies. Older issues of journals can normally be borrowed.

When you borrow items from the library, you should make a note of the 'return' or 'due' date. If you do not return items in time, you will probably have to pay a fine. For short-loan items, fines can be charged by the hour.

Exercise 6

Log on to your library website and look for answers to questions 1–5.

1   How many items can you borrow at once?

2   How long can you borrow items for?

3   Can you reserve or renew items online?

4   Are fines charged for overdue items? If so, what is the rate?

5   How do you request an inter-library loan?

Using a database

A database is an electronic catalogue or list of published materials. Library catalogues are databases; however, library catalogues have two main limitations: they only list items available in the library and they do not normally list articles separately. If you only have the name of an article or you want to know what publications are available on a particular topic, you need to use another database. There are general databases, such as JSTOR or ArticleFirst, which list publications on a wide variety of subjects. There are also specialist databases which list items relating to specific subjects or academic disciplines.

Academic databases are very useful for essays, because they only include items that are 'peer reviewed', that is, judged to be academically credible by other experts. Another advantage of databases is that they often provide not just the bibliographic information about the article (the title, author, year and so on) but also a short summary of the article contents. This is called an abstract.

For more information on abstracts, see Chapter 4.

You can use open access databases, that is, databases that are available to the general public through the internet, or subscribe to particular databases yourself. However, in most cases, it is easiest to access databases through your university library catalogue. Your library will probably subscribe to many different databases. You can search the databases to see what has been published on your topic, and then check your library catalogue to see if the items you want are available in your library. If your library does not stock an item, you may be able to obtain it through an inter-library loan.

If you know which databases you want, search for them by title. Check your course reading list or ask a librarian for recommended databases for your subject. If you do not know which databases to use, search for them by subject. For example, if you are looking for information about how children learn to read, you could look for databases under *education*.

When you have selected the database you want to use, you can search for items in the same way that you search your library catalogue: by title, author and key words. However, as with e-book and e-journal providers, each database has its own website so they all look and work slightly differently.

Advanced keyword searches

Searching for items in a database requires a lot of skill and practice. There are several ways in which you can make keyword searches more efficient.

Searching for phrases

For most databases, if you wish to search for a phrase, rather than individual key words, you can place quotation marks ("...") around the phrase. For example if you are looking for articles for the essay question: *Examine the impact of management style on teamwork in organizations,* you can type "management style" in the search box. The database will list all of the articles containing that phrase. If you type the words in without quotation marks, the database will list all of the articles that contain the words *management* and *style* in separate places. You may end up with a list containing many irrelevant articles, for example articles about style in fashion or architecture.

Exercise 7

Look at essay questions 1–4. Put quotation marks around the phrases you would use in a key word search.

1   Critically evaluate media coverage of the 2008 banking crisis.

2   Relate the principal factors that are commonly thought to influence a person's choice of life partner to Abraham Maslow's hierarchy of needs.

3   Compare and contrast electricity generation from wind power versus electricity generation from hydropower in terms of efficiency, value for money and environmental impact.

4   How does online social networking affect the way adolescents form friendships?

Truncation

Another technique that you can use to search more efficiently is to truncate key words so that articles containing words in the same word family are also listed in your search result. For example, if you are looking for articles about banking crises, you can truncate the word *banking* by typing a * after the root *bank*: bank*. This will ensure that articles containing the words *bank*, *banks*, *bank's* and *banking* will appear in your search results.

Exercise 8

Truncate one word in each of the phrases 1–3. What additional words would be included in the search?

1   environmental impact

2   online social networking

3   form friendships

Boolean operators

A third way of making your search more efficient is to use 'Boolean operators'. This involves combining your key words using 'and', 'or' and 'not' to make your search either more specific or more general. For example, if you want only articles that discuss both children and adolescents, enter 'children *and* adolescents'. The more words you join with 'and', the smaller the number of results. Entering 'children *and* adolescents *and* friendship' will only get you articles that discuss both children and adolescents in relation to friendship.

If you want to widen your search results, use 'or'. For example if you want all of the articles that discuss only children as well as all of the articles that discuss only adolescents, you should search for 'children *or* adolescents'. 'Or' is also useful for entering synonyms into your search. If the topic you are interested in is commonly referred to in a number of ways, you should use 'or' to capture as many relevant articles as possible. Some authors, for example, may use the word *teenager* instead of *adolescent*. In this case, you should search for 'adolescents *or* teenagers'. The more words you join with 'or' the larger the number of results.

It is common to combine 'or' and 'and' operators. For example, if you are interested in how adolescents form friendships, you might search for: 'adolescents *or* teenagers *and* friendship'. Note: for some databases, you need to put terms you want to connect by 'or' in brackets, for example: '(adolescents *or* teenagers) *and* friendship'.

Using the operator 'not' narrows your search by excluding any article with the word or phrase which follows 'not'. This is useful when one of your key words has multiple meanings. For example the word *capital* can mean a sum of money or it can refer to a city where government is based. If you are only interested in the first meaning, you can enter 'capital *not* city'. This makes it more likely that your results will only include articles relating to finance.

Search screens vary in format, so in some cases you may need to type in the operators yourself, in others you may select them from a drop down menu. Spend some time practising using different databases or search engines.

Tips Use Boolean operators to refine your key word searches.
  ✓ Use 'and' to combine key words and narrow your results.
  ✓ Use 'or' to include synonyms for key words and widen your results.
  ✓ Use 'not' to exclude irrelevant items.

Exercise 9

Prepare to do a key word search of the essay question: *Is generosity an innate human trait?* by following steps 1–4 below.

1   Underline the key words.

2   Write a synonym for *generosity*.

3   Decide where to use quotation marks to indicate a phrase.

4   Write your search terms using the Boolean operators 'or' and 'and'.

Making the most of the library

As more and more information becomes available online, you may be tempted to do all of your research by computer and avoid your university library altogether. However, if you do this, you will miss out on a very useful resource. In addition to print and electronic copies of books and academic journals, your library is likely to have:

- specialist librarians who can give you advice on resources in your subject area

- training courses on using library facilities such as databases

- quiet study spaces

- printing, photocopying and IT facilities

- access to inter-library loans.

Using the internet for research

Glossary

bias
Bias is a tendency to prefer one person or thing to another, and to favour that person or thing.

If you do not have access to a library, searching for information on the internet using a search engine such as Google ™ can be a good option. Remember that the internet contains vast amounts of information, so good key word search skills are essential. Most search engines have advanced search options which allow you to use Boolean operators to narrow down your search. Sometimes these may appear as options such as 'any of these words' (= and) or 'all of these words' (= or).

When you search the internet, you also need to be able to identify academically credible sources within your search results. Whereas library catalogues and academic databases contain items which have been selected for their academic credibility, internet search results will automatically list any online material which contains your search terms. In addition, most web search engines are commercial businesses which rely on income from advertising. Companies may pay to have their web pages ranked higher in search results or to have their web pages advertised alongside. This means that you need to look carefully for commercial bias when selecting information for your essay.

Using a specialized search engine facility such as Google Scholar ™ can help because it lists scholarly publications such as journal articles, books, theses and so on; however, you still need to evaluate the source of the items you find listed.

For more information on choosing suitably academic material, see Chapter 3.

Exercise 10

Enter the search terms 'generosity' and 'innate human trait' into Google ™ and Google Scholar™ and compare the first ten items returned by each search result. How many of the items appear to be scholarly?

Remember

✓ When looking for information for an essay, begin with sources listed in your course reading lists and handouts.

✓ Learn to use your university library catalogue.

✓ Get to know where print books and journals in your subject are shelved.

✓ Make sure you know your institutional login so that you can access e-journals and e-books held by your library.

✓ Find out what academic databases are recommended for your subject.

✓ Learn to refine key word searches by using phrases, truncation and Boolean operators.

✓ Find out what additional services your library has to offer – take advantage of any training available.

✓ When using the internet for research, narrow your key word searches and be prepared to evaluate items listed in your results for academic credibility.

3 Choosing the right source material

Aims ✓ choose academically credible
materials

✓ know who the experts are

✓ recognize what makes a text
academic

✓ choose relevant materials

✓ manage your materials

Aims

? Quiz
Self-evaluation

Which of these texts are suitable to use when writing an essay? Circle your
answer.

1	An online encyclopaedia entry	OK | not OK | not sure
2	A textbook	OK | not OK | not sure
3	A newspaper article	OK | not OK | not sure
4	Lecture notes	OK | not OK | not sure
5	An article from a magazine	OK | not OK | not sure
6	An online lecture	OK | not OK | not sure

Choosing academically credible source material for your essay

Glossary

source material
Source materials
are books,
articles, and
other documents
that provide
information for a
piece of research.

Selecting good quality source material for your essay is a key skill.
Relying on materials recommended in your course reading list is a safe
option, but it may not give you all the information you need. You will
have to develop the ability to select the right type of material yourself.
This is particularly important if you use the internet for research.

Advances in information technology have increased the amount of
information available but made it more difficult to identify good quality
material. It is now possible for virtually anyone with access to the
internet to make their writing available to the public. Whereas in the past,
publishers and librarians would have screened information for quality,
now the researcher is largely responsible for this task.

Glossary

screen
If you screen something, you check it systematically to decide whether it is suitable.

cite
If you cite something, you quote it or mention it, especially as an example or proof of what you are saying.

Some sources, academic journal articles for example, are normally considered more academically acceptable than newspaper articles for example. However, what is acceptable for your essay will depend on your topic and how you intend to use the material. If, for example, you are writing an essay analysing media coverage of the 2008 banking crisis, it would not only be appropriate but also necessary to refer to newspaper articles and news broadcasts. Nevertheless, you would also need to find sources that support your observations and ideas about the media coverage. To do this, you need to find academically credible source materials.

There are many different types of materials available, each with advantages and disadvantages. Although some sources of information may not be sufficiently rigorous for you to cite in your essay, they may be useful to you in other ways as you do your research. Popular magazines such as *The Economist* or *New Scientist,* for example, could give you a readable introduction to a topic and ideas that you can then go on to investigate through more academic sources if required.

Exercise 1

Match each type of material 1–6 with the comment a–f that you think best fits.

Type of material	Lecturers' thoughts on academic credibility
1 Online encyclopaedias (for example, Wikipedia™)	a 'These rate highly in terms of academic credibility and up-to-date developments in the field, but they can be very technical, highly specialized and difficult to read.'
2 Newspapers (for example, *The Times*)	b 'These can give you a useful overview of the subject and are academically credible. They are bulky but generally easy to read as they have been written for learners.'
3 Academic journals	c 'These books are often fun and possibly interesting to read but not usually considered appropriate academic sources. Issues are often presented in a subjective and entertaining way to maximize sales.'
4 Lecture notes	d 'Anyone can write articles for these. The information is not peer-reviewed, so it may be biased, subjective or inaccurate. But they can be useful for a quick overview of the subject and are easy to access if you have a computer.'
5 Popular books	e 'The information is up-to-date but may have been hastily researched and/or sensationalized. Not generally considered academically credible.'
6 Textbooks	f 'It's OK to cite this source from time to time, so long as you demonstrate that you've thought critically about it. Lecturers generally don't like having their words quoted back to them as if they were the absolute truth.'

Knowing who the experts are

Before you spend time reading a text, it is normally a good idea to check the author's credentials. Authors of good quality, reliable information generally:

- have professional qualifications showing they have the knowledge and training to write about the topic

- are connected to or work for a recognized and respected organization, for example a university, a research institute, a government department, or professional association

- have their work published by recognized publishing houses, journals or organizations

- are cited in other academic works

- do not gain commercial advantage through promoting certain views.

Tips
- ✓ If you are not sure whether a publisher, journal or organization is suitable, ask your lecturer and/or university librarian for advice.
- ✓ If you do not know whether the author of a book or article has been cited in other academic works, check the bibliographies of related publications.
- ✓ Search for the item through Google Scholar™, which shows how often publications have been cited in other academic literature.

Exercise 2

Read the following biographical information about an author.

Does the author appear to have suitable academic credentials? Why or why not?

'Heidi Cullen is a senior research scientist with Climate Central, a non-profit research organization through which she reports on climate change for news outlets, including *PBS NewsHour*, Time.com and The Weather Channel. Before joining Climate Central, Dr. Cullen served as The Weather Channel's first on-air climate expert and helped create *Forecast Earth*, the first weekly television series to focus on issues related to climate change and the environment. She is a visiting lecturer at Princeton University, a member of the American Geophysical Union and American Meteorological Society, and an associate editor of the journal *Weather, Climate, and Society* [...] She holds a BS in engineering and a PhD in climatology from Columbia University and lives with her husband and two dogs in Princeton, New Jersey.'

Source: Extract "About the Author" from *The Weather of the Future* by Heidi Cullen. Copyright © 2010 by Heidi Cullen.

Tips   ✓ Use educational and government websites with internet suffixes: .edu, .ac or .gov as they are generally considered more credible.

✓ Avoid online material that is published through commercial sites (sites with a .com or .co suffix) as they may be biased.

✓ Websites of non-commercial organizations usually have a .org suffix. Cite widely known and respected organizations, such as the United Nations.

✓ Be wary of other organizations set up to promote a particular view or cause. They may be biased so indicate this possibility in your essay if you cite them.

Exercise 3

A student searching the internet for texts for the essay: *Is generosity an innate human trait?* came up with the search results below. Which of the items should be treated with caution? Why?

1 Is altruism a genetic trait?: Scientific American	http://www.scientificamerican.com
2 BBC NEWS | Science/Nature | Altruism 'in-built' in humans	http://news.bbc.co.uk
3 Evolution of morality – Wikipedia, the free encyclopedia	http://en.wikipedia.org
4 The natural selection of altruistic traits	http://courses.washington.edu
5 Altruism essays	http://www.megaessays.com

Choosing up-to-date materials

Glossary

seminal
A seminal work is an important and influential work.

It is generally preferable to use up-to-date source materials, ideally published within the last five years. However, what 'up-to-date' means in practice depends on your topic. If you are researching a topic that is changing rapidly, for example topics related to science, engineering and information technology, books and articles even a few years old may no longer be relevant.

Sometimes, on the other hand, it may be acceptable or even necessary to refer to older source material, for example, if you are referring to a seminal work or if you are giving a historical overview of what scholars have said about your topic.

Recognizing academic texts

From time to time you will come across texts which appear to be written by authors with academic credentials but which are still not appropriate for use in your essay because they have not been written for a scholarly audience. It is therefore important to be able to recognize whether a text is appropriate by looking at the way it is written.

Exercise 4

Read the text below. Do you think it has been written for an academic audience? Why or why not?

'We've all had experience of generous behaviour – people helping others without expecting something in return. We naturally assume that altruism is a virtue that we learn from our parents when we are children. 'Share your toys … Be nice … Let your little brother go first …' But science says that altruism is probably instinctive.

Fascinating studies of the chimp, our closest relative, have produced evidence that altruism is a genetic trait. Chimps don't teach their offspring to be generous, but scientists Felix Warneken and Michael Tomasello from the Max Planck Institute for Evolutionary Anthropology in Leipzig, Germany have discovered that chimps do give other chimps a hand, even ones they don't know, without expecting a reward.'

Glossary

noun phrase
A noun phrase is a noun or pronoun, or a group of words based on a noun or pronoun.

When authors write in an academic style for an academic audience, they are more likely to:

- support opinions with evidence

- refer to other authors by surname (for example, 'Davis' rather than 'John Davis' or 'Mr Davis')

- give bibliographic information about works cited (for example, 'Davis (2009: 24) states that …'

- use 'objective' language (for example, 'It is often said that …' rather than 'We often say that …'

- use formal language (for example 'numerous' rather than 'lots of')

- use precise language

- use noun phrases rather than verbs (for example, 'excessive alcohol consumption' rather than 'drinking too much alcohol') and less likely to:

- make claims that are not backed up by evidence

- make exaggerated claims or categorical statements, that is statements that do not have exceptions (for example 'everyone likes to have fun')

- refer to other authors by their full names or first names, or use titles such as 'Dr' or 'Mrs'

- use emotive words, for example 'fantastic', 'dreadful'

- use personal pronouns 'I' and 'you'

- use slang or informal expressions

- use contractions such as 'isn't' or 'won't'

- begin sentences with 'and' or 'but'

- use certain punctuation marks such as the dash (-) or the exclamation mark (!).

Exercise 5

Look again at the text in Exercise 4 and identify the features that make it relatively informal in style.

1   What personal pronouns does the writer use?

2   How does the writer refer to other researchers?

3   What forms of punctuation are there that do not normally appear in more formal texts?

4   What contractions does the writer use?

5   Which words have been abbreviated?

6   Does the writer use any vague or imprecise expressions? If so, what are they?

7   Does the writer use language that is informal or emotive? If so, what examples can you find?

8   What categorical expression does the writer use?

Now compare it with the text below, which has been written in a more academic style.

Altruistic behaviour, that is the offer of assistance to others without the motive of personal gain, is often said to be a characteristically human trait (Carter, 1989; Ericson, 1994). Moreover, it is commonly assumed that children learn to behave altruistically from their parents (Carter, 2004). However, the findings of recent studies of chimpanzee behaviour suggest that altruism may be more instinctive than previously thought. Warneken and Tomasello (2006), for example, have documented numerous instances of chimpanzees assisting other chimpanzees to locate a food source without the expectation of a reward.

Choosing relevant materials

The availability of so much information also means that it is important to learn how to quickly identify whether a text is relevant to your research topic. Titles of academic texts are often very descriptive of their contents, so that is a good place to start. For example, the article from Exercise 3 entitled 'Is altruism a genetic trait?' is based on a research article which has the longer more descriptive title: 'Altruistic Helping in Human Infants and Young Chimpanzees'.

Exercise 6

Imagine you are looking for information to answer the essay question *Assess the European Central Bank's response to the 2008 global financial crisis.* Your key word search has returned the following items. Which items do you think are relevant? Which are not? Why not?

Remember to look carefully at the essay question to identify the focus of your research. Notice how the instructions set the limits of your investigation in terms of

- place

- time

- aspect of the topic to be discussed

1   International financial crises: causes, prevention, and cures

L.H. (2000) *The American Economic Review*, 2000 – JSTOR

2   The aftermath of financial crises

Reinhart, C.M. & Rogoff, K.S. - 2009 - nber.org

3   Structural causes of the global financial crisis: a critical assessment of the 'new financial architecture'

Crotty, I (2009) *Cambridge Journal of Economics*. CPES

4   The regulatory response to the financial crisis

Goodhart, C.A.E (2008) *Journal of Financial Stability*. Elsevier

5   [BOOK] Naudé, W.A. (2009) *The financial crisis of 2008 and the developing countries* - econ.tu.ac.th

Using abstracts to choose relevant articles

Most databases will supply the abstract of articles as well as bibliographic information. Reading abstracts is a very useful way of determining whether an article is relevant to your topic.

Exercise 7

Imagine that you have been asked to research the impact of social networking sites on the psychological health of young people between the ages of 12 and 16. Is the abstract below a useful source of information? Why or why not?

Facebook, as one of the most popular social networking sites among college students, provides a platform for people to manage others' impressions of them. People tend to present themselves in a favorable way on their Facebook profile. This research examines the impact of using Facebook on people's perceptions of others' lives. It is argued that those with deeper involvement with Facebook will have different perceptions of others than those less involved due to two reasons. First, Facebook users tend to base judgment on examples easily recalled (the availability heuristic). Second, Facebook users tend to attribute the positive content presented on Facebook to others' personality, rather than situational factors (correspondence bias), especially for those they do not know personally. Questionnaires, including items measuring years of using Facebook, time spent on Facebook each week, number of people listed as their Facebook "friends", and perceptions about others' lives, were completed by 425 undergraduate students taking classes across various academic disciplines at a state university in Utah. Surveys were collected during regular class period, except for two online classes where surveys were submitted online. The multivariate analysis indicated that those who have used Facebook longer agreed more that others were happier, and agreed less that life is fair, and those spending more time on Facebook each week agreed more that others were happier and had better lives. Furthermore, those that included more people whom they did not personally know as their Facebook "friends" agreed more that others had better lives. (246 words)

Source: Chou, H. G., & Edge, N. (2012). "They Are Happier and Having Better Lives than I Am": The Impact of Using Facebook on Perceptions of Others' Lives. *Cyberpsychology, Behavior, and Social Networking, 15(2), 117–121.*

To determine whether a book is relevant to your topic, check the back cover or inside the front cover for a summary of the contents. If this is not present, or if it does not give you enough information to decide whether the book is relevant, you may need to survey the book or article to verify that it contains information that you are looking for.

For more information on abstracts and on surveying, see Chapter 4.

Managing your materials

Glossary

repository
A repository is
a place where
something is
kept safely.

As you do your research, it is important to have a good system for storing your source materials. Remember that items you have borrowed from the library may be recalled by other users, so where possible photocopy the material that you need. Make sure you respect copyright law. Tagging items with a note of why you selected it or what you intend to use it for may be useful. Keep all paper copies of items in one place.

For online materials, use the 'favourites' function in your computer or consider using programs which allow you to save different types of files including web pages, PDFs, and audio files into a single file. Many such programs allow you to store your material in a web-based repository, so even if your computer breaks down or is lost, your files can be retrieved.

However you choose to store your source materials make sure that you have full bibliographic information for each item. This will make it easier to create an alphabetical list of sources for the end of your essay.

For books, the bibliographic information you need to record includes:

- the author or authors if there are more than one, keeping the names in the same order in which they appear on the cover

- the date (use the date of the edition you are using, disregard dates of reprints)

- the title (and edition if relevant)

- the publisher

- the place of publication (usually the city).

If you have consulted a chapter within an edited volume, you also need to record the author and title of the chapter, the name of the editor(s) and the title of the book, and the page numbers of the chapter (first and last).

For journal articles, you need to record:

- the author or authors if there are more than one, keeping the names in the same order in which they appear

- the date

- the title of the article

- the title of the journal

- the volume and issue number

- the page numbers (first and last) of the article.

For online materials, you should also record the URL and the date that you accessed the material.

Tip   ✓   If you are working on paper, record the bibliographic details of each source on a separate index card or sheet of paper.

Tip

For more examples of bibliographic entries, see Chapter 11; for more on copyright law, see Chapter 2; for more on making notes, see Chapter 8.

Remember

✓   Choose materials written by authors with suitable academic or professional credentials.

✓   Choose materials that have been written in an academic style for an academic audience.

✓   When searching on the internet, choose materials from .edu, .ac, or .gov sites.

✓   Choose up-to-date texts, unless you have a good reason to refer to older sources.

✓   To help you decide whether a book is relevant to your topic, skim read the back cover, table of contents, index and introduction.

✓   To help you decide whether an article is relevant, read the abstract.

✓   If the material you have is too difficult to read, familiarize yourself with the topic by reading texts written for a general audience.

✓   Keep a full bibliographic record of everything you have read for your topic.

4 | Academic texts

? Quiz
Self-evaluation

How confident do you feel about reading the types of texts below? Rate each one from 1 = not at all confident to 5 = very confident.

1	A textbook (= a book containing facts about a particular subject)	
2	A monograph (= a book which is a detailed study of only one subject)	
3	A journal article (= a piece of writing in a magazine which deals with a specialized subject)	
4	A report (= an official document produced after investigating something)	

Types of academic texts

Glossary

commentary
A commentary is an article or book which explains or discusses something.

Source texts can be classified in different ways. One common way is to divide them into 'primary' and 'secondary' sources. Primary sources are original materials on which other research is based. These might include letters, government documents, works of literature and so on. Secondary sources are commentaries or interpretations of primary sources. Textbooks are normally considered secondary sources as are most other books and articles which are the products of research. Depending on your subject discipline, you may need to read secondary sources only, or a combination of secondary and primary sources.

Primary source texts vary enormously and can take many different forms; however, the types of secondary sources you are likely to use in your research have some predictable features. As you become more familiar with these features, it will become easier for you to read them and find the information you need.

Textbooks

It is often a good idea to start your research by looking at textbooks. Textbooks are written specifically for learners, and are designed to be easy to read. Paragraphs are often clearly structured with topic sentences and clear examples to illustrate the points made. Key words are frequently defined within the text or listed in a glossary. Chapters typically begin with a statement of aims and conclude with summaries and/or questions for reflection. Textbook writers also use a number of strategies for making important information stand out:

- Headings and subheadings

- Bold, italicized or coloured fonts for key words and concepts

- Bulleted or numbered lists

- Pictures and diagrams

- Text boxes

You can use these features, along with the table of contents and index to help you survey the text before you read it in detail. Surveying the text will help you:

- identify which parts are relevant to your essay topic

- give you a mental map of the text so that you can understand the detailed information more easily

- stimulate your curiosity by giving you 'clues' about the contents – this can help you read more actively and with greater focus.

Exercise 1

This book has also been designed to assist learning. What features can you identify that make this a 'learner-friendly' text?

Exercise 2

Choose a textbook related to your subject of study. Select a chapter and read only those parts that are designed to stand out, starting with the chapter summary, if there is one. Focus on:

a   headings and subheadings

b   information in bold, coloured or italicized fonts

c   lists

d   pictures and diagrams

e   text boxes

Try to form a mental map of how the information is laid out. Then read the chapter from start to finish and answer questions 1–3.

1   Which of the features a–e did you find?

2   Which features were most useful in drawing your attention to important information?

3   To what extent did surveying the chapter help you understand the content?

Try reading a chapter without surveying it first and compare your experience.

Monographs

Glossary

substantial
Substantial means large in amount or degree.

A monograph is an in-depth study of a specialized topic. Monographs can be challenging to read because they often require substantial background knowledge. Also, there is no set or typical pattern of organization for this type of book.

Before investing your time in reading an entire book, it is important to survey the text to determine whether it is relevant to your essay. Surveying the book will also allow you to check whether the material is too dense or difficult for you to read. If most of the sentences you read contain words that are unfamiliar to you, you may be better off looking for an easier text.

Begin by looking at the back cover, which may give a brief summary of its contents, and then the table of contents. Sometimes the order of chapters will give you an idea of the author's argument or 'line of reasoning'. Scan the index, if there is one, for key words related to your topic and note the page numbers.

Begin by looking at the back cover, which may give a brief summary of its contents, and then the table of contents. Sometimes the order of chapters will give you an idea of the author's argument or 'line of reasoning'. Scan the index, if there is one, for key words related to your topic and note the page numbers.

For more information on scanning, see Chapter 5.

Next read the introduction for information about the author's aims and how the book is structured. This information often comes towards the end of the introduction.

Once you have a reasonable understanding of the writer's aims and line of argument, you can focus on those chapters which are most likely to contain the information relevant to your essay. Remember that, because academic monographs are often difficult to read, you may need to use a variety of strategies to help you understand the information.

If you own the book or you have a photocopy of the parts you want to read, you can use a marker to annotate it with the features that are commonly found in textbooks to make the key information stand out.

- Highlight the writer's aims.

- Highlight key words and write their definitions in the margins.

- If there are no section headings, add them yourself in the margins.

- Number key points or stages in the argument.

- Draw boxes around the most important passages.

Glossary

scan
When you scan written material, you look through it quickly in order to find important or interesting information.

annotate
If you annotate written work or a diagram, you add notes to it, especially in order to explain it.

Exercise 3

Photocopy a section of a book related to your essay topic. Practise annotating it in the ways suggested above. Look at the text again after a few days, focussing on your annotations. Answer questions 1–3.

1   To what extent do your annotations help you recall the information?

2   Which of your annotations are most useful?

3   What changes (if any) would you make to your annotations to make them more effective?

Edited books

Books consisting of chapters written by different authors (or groups of authors) are called 'edited' books or volumes. An edited book is put together by one or more editors who write the introduction, sometimes called a 'preface'. The introduction gives information about the subject, aims and scope of the book. Often brief summaries of the chapters are provided along with explanations of why they have been chosen. These can help you choose what to read.

Edited books can be particularly useful to you when you are researching an essay. Firstly, the texts have often been brought together because they offer different perspectives on the topic. This is important if you are thinking, and writing, critically about your subject. Secondly, the chapters are often reprints of articles which have been written by experts in the field and previously published in journals. Articles reprinted in this way are often considered to be important or influential.

The organization and typical features of chapters within edited books can vary enormously. However, on the whole they can be approached in the same way that you would approach a journal article.

Empirical journal articles

Journal articles can be broadly categorized into two main types: empirical or source based. Even if you do not have to read journal articles for your essay, it is useful to know how they are structured because they are often summarized and/or referred to in textbooks.

Empirical articles report on research studies which are based on observation or experimentation. They are common in the sciences and social sciences. Most empirical articles follow a standard structure, commonly referred to as IMRAD, which stands for Introduction, Methods, Results and Discussion. They contain the following elements:

Title – The title usually describes the focus of the paper and contains carefully chosen key words. This ensures that the article will appear in the database search results of other researchers looking for information about the topic.

Glossary

corroborate
To corroborate something that has been said or reported means to provide evidence or information that supports it.

A **hypothesis** is an idea which is suggested as a possible explanation for a particular situation or condition, but has not yet been proved to be correct.

rationale
The rationale for a course of action, practice, or belief is the set of reasons on which it is based.

validity
The validity of something such as a result or a piece of information is whether it can be trusted or believed.

replicate
If you replicate someone's experiment, work, or research, you do it yourself in exactly the same way.

Author(s) – Empirical research articles are often written by teams of researchers. The name of the researcher who has made the greatest contribution usually appears first in the list. The authors' affiliations are also given making it easy to evaluate their credentials.

Abstract – The abstract gives a summary of the article and is normally between 150 and 250 words long. The structure of the abstract usually follows the structure of the paper.

Introduction – The main purpose of the introduction is to present the context of the research and explain why the research has been done. The introduction usually states the topic of the paper, gives a review of previous research on the topic (usually referred to as a 'literature review'), and explains how the article relates to that research. The article is usually described as corroborating previous research, extending previous research, or challenging previous research. The researchers will usually state the key research question or questions they are trying to answer. In some papers, this is presented as hypotheses. Sometimes introductions will contain a summary of the most important results or 'findings'.

Methods – In the methods section the researchers describe how the research was done. They provide information about the materials or subjects used and the procedures followed. They also normally give a rationale for their choice of methods as well as an explanation of how the findings were analysed. This information is important because it allows other scholars to judge the validity of the results and/or replicate the study.

Results – In this section, the findings are presented, often in the form of graphs and tables. The key findings are described and highlighted in the accompanying text but generally not interpreted.

Discussion – In the discussion section, the researchers explain their findings. They indicate the extent to which their findings answer the research questions they posed in the introduction. They offer an interpretation of their findings and an assessment of their significance in relation to previous research. Recommendations for future research are also made. Sometimes there is a separate conclusion section in which the main points are emphasized and recommendations are made.

Exercise 4

Extracts 1–4 below have been reprinted from the abstract to a journal article. Indicate whether each extract refers to the introduction, methods, results or discussion section of the article. In what order did the sentences appear in the abstract?

1   We argue that this effect may be the result of a feedback loop whereby using Facebook exposes people to often ambiguous information about their partner that they may not otherwise have access to and that this new information incites further Facebook use. Our study provides evidence of Facebook's unique contributions to the experience of jealousy in romantic relationships.

2   The social network site Facebook is a rapidly expanding phenomenon that is changing the nature of social relationships. Anecdotal evidence, including information described in the popular media, suggests that Facebook may be responsible for creating jealousy and suspicion in romantic relationships. The objectives of the present study were to explore the role of Facebook in the experience of jealousy and to determine if increased Facebook exposure predicts jealousy above and beyond personal and relationship factors.

3   Three hundred eight undergraduate students completed an online survey that assessed demographic and personality factors and explored respondents' Facebook use.

4   A hierarchical multiple regression analysis, controlling for individual, personality, and relationship factors, revealed that increased Facebook use significantly predicts Facebook-related jealousy.

Source: Extract from Muise, A., Christofides, E., & Desmarais, S. (2009). More Information than You Ever Wanted: Does Facebook Bring Out the Green-Eyed Monster of Jealousy? *CyberPsychology & Behavior, 12(4)*, 441–444.

Empirical journal articles are often relatively long and can be difficult to read. In many cases you will not need to read the whole article in detail in order to find the information you need for your essay.

Tips   To access the most important information first, read the sections of an empirical journal article in the following way:

✓   read the abstract carefully
✓   read the introduction relatively quickly
✓   look briefly at the graphs and tables in the results section
✓   read the discussion (or conclusion) carefully
✓   skim the methods section.

Source-based journal articles

Glossary

theoretical perspective
If you examine something from a theoretical perspective, you consider the ideas and abstract principles relating to it rather than its practical aspects or uses.

The other broad category of journal articles can be described as source-based. These are commonly found in the humanities and social sciences, such as history, languages, or sociology.

This type of article varies widely in form and does not follow any set pattern. However, it generally interprets some aspect of culture or society by examining it from a theoretical perspective. The purpose is not to solve a particular problem or reach a definitive conclusion, but to expand the debate around the topic under consideration.

When students write essays based on source materials they are essentially training to write this type of article. Therefore many of the criteria used to judge student essays are present in source-based journal articles.

Tips When reading a source-based journal article, it is often helpful to ask yourself the following questions:

✓ What theme, issue or question is the author seeking to explore?
✓ What is the author's theoretical perspective?
✓ What new understanding or 'insights' do we gain by looking at the topic in this way?

Exercise 5

Read the abstract below from an article. Then answer the questions in the Tips box above.

This paper analyzes four animated films in order to explore themes of leadership crises and leadership emergence. Drawing on psychoanalysis and structuralist film studies, this paper explores leadership emergence as mythic structure within the four films, arguing that these myths are structured around a struggle of a young novice against an evil power figure, and the overcoming of this figure through a process of self-discovery and maturation. Central themes include the relations between self-realization of leaders and the social harmony, the battle with evil leaders as an ego-struggle, and exile and journey as a precursor to mature leadership competence. [...] More generally, it is argued that treating popular culture such as animated allegories as contemporary myth offers scholars a view into popular conceptions of leadership, possibly illuminating the relationships between leadership and social organization.

Source: Extract from Animating Leadership: Crisis and renewal of governance in 4 mythic narratives by Islam, G. (2009). *The Leadership Quarterly, 20(5)*, 828–836.

Reports

If you are studying a subject that has a strong practical focus, for example engineering, business, or public policy, you may be required to refer to professional reports. These are generally written by professionals or academics, often with the aim of providing practical solutions to a problem. The intended readers might be academics but are more likely to be decision makers or professionals in the field.

Reports can be long and detailed. However, they usually follow a fairly standard form within each discipline and contain features that make them easy to read quickly. A typical report is likely to have elements which are similar to the elements found in an empirical journal article. There is generally:

- a brief but descriptive title

- an abstract or executive summary

- an introduction explaining the context, the reason for the report, and how the investigation was done

- the main text, often clearly divided into sections, where the findings are described, analysed and evaluated

- conclusions and recommendations which specify what actions should be taken.

Exercise 6

Look at the headings of a report on the funding of older people's social care in the United Kingdom. Which section do you think most clearly describes a problem? Which sections probably describe solutions?

Care in Crisis 2012

Summary

1   Introduction

2   The funding crisis to date

3   Tracking the effect of government spending

4   The architecture of reform

5   Future funding of care

References

Source: Extract from Care in Crisis 2012.
http://www.ageuk.org.uk/get-involved/campaign/poor-quality-care-services-big-q/care-in-crisis-2012-report/

Like empirical research articles, reports can often be read selectively. Start by getting the main ideas, then read as much of the detail as you need to for your particular essay. Often, it is sufficient to focus on the executive summary, headings, introduction and recommendations.

Remember

✓ Begin your research by reading learner-friendly texts, such as textbooks.

✓ Before reading a textbook chapter in detail, survey it by looking first at the elements that have been designed to stand out: headings, italicized words, diagrams and so on.

✓ Where possible, read selectively from single-author academic books – survey the back cover, table of contents and the introduction to find the most useful sections.

✓ Use edited volumes to read about your subject from different perspectives.

✓ To read an empirical journal article, focus on the abstract, the introduction, tables and figures, and the discussion or conclusion. Read the other sections if necessary.

✓ To read a source-based journal article, focus on identifying the issue, the author's theoretical perspective, and the new understanding or interpretation put forward.

✓ Where possible, read selectively from reports – focus on the headings, executive summary, introduction, conclusion and recommendations. Read the other sections if necessary.

5 | Reading strategies

Aims ✓ choose the right reading strategy for your purpose ✓ read quickly for specific information
✓ read quickly for a general overview ✓ deal with unfamiliar vocabulary
✓ read complex and difficult sentences

Aims

? Quiz
Self-evaluation

Read the statements, then circle the word which is true for you.

1	I can use a variety of reading strategies, depending on what I need.	agree | disagree | not sure
2	I can read quickly to get the main idea of a text.	agree | disagree | not sure
3	I can read quickly to locate specific information in a text.	agree | disagree | not sure
4	I have a variety of strategies to help me understand new vocabulary.	agree | disagree | not sure
5	I use techniques to help me understand complex and difficult texts.	agree | disagree | not sure

What are reading strategies and why should you use them?

In simple terms, reading strategies are plans that we carry out to achieve certain reading goals. When we think of reading, we often think of it as a single activity: we read a text from start to finish in order to understand the information in it. But in fact, we read texts in many different ways using a variety of reading strategies, though we might not always realize it.

This is particularly true when you are doing something as complex as research. When you read an online search results page in order to find articles for an essay, you are probably going to read in a particular way – perhaps running your eyes quickly down the list looking for words related to your topic.

If, on the other hand, you are reading a text explaining a theory that you want to apply in your essay, you are probably going to approach it in a very different way – perhaps reading more slowly and carefully pausing frequently to think about what you have read. In fact, when you are researching information for your essay, you will be using a variety of reading strategies to accomplish different reading goals. Through practice, you can become good at these strategies.

Good researchers are not only good at using reading strategies; they are also good at making decisions about when to use a particular strategy. There are many different strategies, and they can be categorized in different ways; here, I have divided them into 'fast' reading strategies and 'intensive' reading strategies.

Fast reading strategies

Fast reading strategies are essential for handling the large amounts of information involved in doing research. You have already been introduced to one fast reading strategy in Chapter 4: surveying the text.

There are several other fast reading strategies that will be useful to you as a researcher.

For more on surveying a text, see Chapter 4.

Skimming

The terms *skimming* and *surveying* are sometimes used interchangeably; however, in this book I use *surveying* to mean reading those parts of the text, such as the table of contents, text boxes, and headings, which stand out from the main text. The main purpose of surveying is to decide if a text is suitable for use. I use the term *skimming* to refer to reading selectively from a text which may not have features such as headings and text boxes. The main purpose of skimming is to get an overview of the content. Surveying and skimming can be done together as they serve similar purposes. They allow you to:

- identify whether a text is relevant
- gain an overview of the author's argument
- identify which parts of a text are most relevant
- prepare yourself for intensive reading.

Skimming can be done in different ways, depending on the type and length of text. To skim a single paragraph, begin by reading the first sentence, which is most likely to state the topic of the paragraph.

Tips If you are not able to identify the main point of the paragraph from the first sentence, or if the first sentence indicates that there is more important information coming, run your eyes quickly over the middle part of the paragraph looking out for:

✓ signposting expressions that signal key points such as 'however' and 'furthermore'
✓ adjectives and adverbs that indicate importance, such as 'significant', 'main' or 'interestingly'.

If these are not present, read the last sentence in the paragraph, which often acts as a conclusion.

Exercise 1

Read the paragraph below about attraction and friendship and answer questions 1 and 2 below.

1 Which sentence most clearly states the main idea?

2 Which words elsewhere in the paragraph indicate that you might want to read more?

'There is a good chance that you will get to like people who are in a reasonable proximity to where you live or work – think of this as the neighbourhood factor. In a famous study of a student housing complex led by Leon Festinger (who is also associated with the concept of cognitive dissonance discussed in Chapter 6), it emerged that people were more likely to choose as friends those living in the same building and even on the same floor. (Festinger, Schachter & Black, 1950). Subtle architectural features, such as the location of a staircase, can also affect the process of making acquaintances and establishing friendships.'

Source: Extracts from Vaughan & Hogg, Psychology © 2011 Pearson Australia pp 544–545, 537–538, 498.

To skim a longer text which is divided into paragraphs, you normally read:

■ the first paragraph (or introductory section) completely

■ the first sentence or line of each paragraph in the main body of the text

■ the last paragraph (or concluding section) completely.

Exercise 2

Imagine that you are researching the factors that influence a person's choice of life partner and that you have found the text below. The first and last paragraphs have been reproduced along with the first sentences of the middle five paragraphs. Read the extracts and answer questions 1–4.

1   Is this article relevant to your research topic?

2   Do the authors present the theory in a favourable light?

3   Which part of the text might you use to complete the sentence: 'According to social exchange theory, one of the factors that may influence a person's choice of life partner is the extent to which they can exchange resources such as "...."'?

4   Which paragraph would you read completely if you wanted to know more about how people decide whether a relationship is better or worse than other relationships they have had in the past?

'Is there a relationships marketplace out there, where we humans can satisfy our needs to interact, be intimate, 'love and be loved in return'? While social exchange theory is one of a family of theories based on behaviourism, it is also an approach to studying interpersonal relationships that incorporates *interaction*. Further, it deals directly with close relationships.

If two people are to progress in a relationship it will be because they gain from the way that they exchange benefits (i.e. rewards). [...]

A relationship is an ongoing everyday activity. [...]

Broadly speaking, resources exchanged include: goods, information, love, money, services and status (Foa and Foa, 1975). [...]

Thibaut and Kelley's (1959) *The social psychology of groups* was a major work that underpinned much subsequent research. [...]

A final important concept in social exchange theory is the part played by each person's comparison level or CL – a standard against which all of one's relationships are judged. [...]

Does exchange theory have a future? In summary, the answer to this question is yes. A strong feature of exchange theory is that it accommodates variations in relationships, including:

■   differences between people in how they perceive rewards and costs (you might think that free advice from your partner is rewarding, others might not);

■   differences within the person based on varying CLs, both over time and across different contexts (I like companionship, but I prefer to shop for clothes alone).

The theory is frequently used. For example, Rusbult has shown how *investment* includes the way that rewards, costs and CLs are related to both satisfaction and commitment in a relationship (Rusbult, Martz & Agnew, 1998).'

Source: Extracts from Vaughan & Hogg, Psychology © 2011 Pearson Australia pp 544–545, 537–538, 498.

Scanning

If you need to find a specific piece of information quickly, you can scan a text for it. To scan efficiently, decide which text – and which part of the text – is most likely to contain the information you are looking for. If necessary, skim the text first in order to get a mental map of how the information is laid out. Then allow your eyes to quickly run over the surface of the text looking for key words relating to the information you are looking for.

Exercise 3

Imagine that you are continuing your research on the factors that influence a person's choice of life partner and that you are looking for answers to questions 1–3. Scan the text to find the answers. Then answer question 4 at the end of the passage.

1　Which scholar is associated with the 'law of attraction'?

2　When did Newcomb study college students' attitudes and attractions?

3　What does 'reinforcing' mean in this context?

'There are other important psychological factors that exert some control over attraction. In an early study by Theodore Newcomb (1961), students received rent-free housing in return for filling in questionnaires before they arrived about their attitudes and values. Changes in interpersonal attraction were measured over the course of a semester. Initially, attraction went hand-in-hand with proximity – students liked those who lived close by. Then another factor came into play: having compatible attitudes. […]

Newcomb found that, as the semester progressed, the focus shifted to similarity of attitudes. Students with similar pre-acquaintance attitudes became more attractive. This is logical, because in real life it usually takes some time to discover whether or not a housemate thinks and feels in the same way about a variety of social issues.

Byrne and Clore have carried out extensive research dealing with the connection between sharing attitudes with another person and liking them (e.g. Byrne, 1971; Clore & Byrne, 1974). Attitudes that were markedly similar were an important ingredient in maintaining a relationship. The results were so reliable and consistent that Clore (1976) formulated a 'law of attraction' – attraction towards a person bears a linear relationship to the actual proportion of similar attitudes shared with that person. This law was thought to be applicable to more than just attitudes. Anything that other people do that agrees with your perception of things is rewarding, i.e. reinforcing. The more other people agree, the more they act as reinforcers for you and the more you like them. For example, if you suddenly discover that someone you are going out with likes the same obscure rock band as you, your liking for that person will increase.'

Source: Extracts from Vaughan & Hogg, Psychology © 2011 Pearson Australia pp 544–545, 537–538, 498.

4　Imagine you wanted to find out more about proximity as a factor that influences attraction – would you read the section before or after this extract?

You may need to scan at any stage of the research process: early on as you gather background information as well as later as you write your essay. Although you may be thorough in your note taking, often it is not until you write your first draft that the details of your argument come together. At that stage it is not unusual to realize that some of the information you most need you have read somewhere but not noted down. In order to retrieve this information, you will need to scan.

Intensive reading

In many cases, you will have to read texts thoroughly in order to understand the content sufficiently well to include it in your essay. If the text is very dense and/or complex, you will probably need to slow down and use intensive reading strategies to help you make sense of the information. When texts are difficult to read it is often for one or more of the following reasons: the concepts are new, the vocabulary is unfamiliar, or the sentences are long and complex. Trying to deal with all of these challenges at the same time may be unrealistic.

Tip ✓ If a text is difficult to read, read the passage several times, each time focussing on one particular difficulty.

Tip

Exercise 4

Read the extract below. Indicate how difficult it is for you by giving it a number from 1 (=not at all difficult) to 5 (=extremely difficult). Identify which of the reasons listed above poses the greatest challenge for you in relation to the passage.

'When making judgments or forming impressions about others, one common attribution error is the correspondence bias; that is, the tendency to assume that others' actions and words reflect their personality or stable personal disposition, rather than being affected by situational factors. When seeing others' happy pictures posted on Facebook, users might conclude that others are happy, while ignoring the circumstances or situations that made others happy. The correspondence bias is more likely to happen when Facebook users make attributions about people whom they have never met before. They assume that happiness is a stable characteristic of their temperaments and that they are constantly enjoying good lives. For those they do know personally, however, their past interactions with them help Facebook users avoid the trap of correspondence bias and recognize the external factors at work: it is the occasions that make their friends happy.'

Source: Chou, H. G. & Edge, N. (2012). "They Are Happier and Having Better Lives than I Am": The Impact of Using Facebook on Perceptions of Others' Lives. *Cyberpsychology, Behavior, and Social Networking, 15(2),* 117–121.

Strategies for dealing with unfamiliar vocabulary

It is often advisable to try to guess the meaning of unfamiliar vocabulary from context as you read rather than to check every new item in your dictionary. However, if you do not understand enough of the content to guess the meaning, use an alternative strategy: deal with the vocabulary first. Identify all of the words that appear to be key – look in particular at the topic and concluding sentences and near expressions that signal importance. Study their definitions in your dictionary, beginning with the words that appear to be nouns. Where words have multiple definitions, look again at the passage and choose the definition that makes most sense in the context. You may need to look at the sentence in the passage in which the word occurs several times with different definitions in mind. Because some words can have different meanings in everyday English and in specific academic contexts, you may need to use a dictionary specifically related to your subject discipline.

Exercise 5

Look at this sentence taken from Exercise 4 and locate words 1–6 below. For each word, select the definition a or b that best fits the context.

'When making judgments or forming impressions about others, one common attribution error is the correspondence bias; that is, the tendency to assume that others' actions and words reflect their personality or stable personal disposition, rather than being affected by situational factors.'

1	correspondence	**a** communication by an exchange of letters	**b** state of being the same as
2	reflect	**a** to think	**b** to express
3	stable	**a** a type of shelter (n)	**b** unchanging (adj)
4	disposition	**a** a person's usual mood	**b** transferring something to another person
5	trap	**a** a device for catching animals or people which is difficult to avoid or escape	**b** an unpleasant situation
6	external	**a** related to or coming from the outside	**b** related to the visible or surface appearance of something

For more on guessing the meaning of vocabulary from context, see Chapter 6.

Once you have familiarized yourself with the most important vocabulary, go back and re-read the passage as a whole.

Strategies for dealing with unfamiliar concepts

Often dealing with unfamiliar vocabulary helps you to clarify the unfamiliar concepts in the passage. However, sometimes you may find that you understand the words but not the key ideas. For example, in the passage in Exercise 4, you may understand the words: 'attribution' and 'error', but you may not have a sufficiently good understanding of the term 'attribution error' as it is used in the field of psychology to make sense of the passage. In this case, it may be necessary to do some more background reading. Online encyclopaedias can be a quick and easily accessible resource for this type of information. Remember, however, that online encyclopaedias are not always reliable sources of information. Although they may be useful for giving you a basic introduction to a concept, you should not use them as sources for your essay.

Exercise 6

Read the entry for 'attribution error' from the online encyclopaedia 'Wikipedia'. In what ways might it help further your understanding of the passage by Chou and Edge?

'In social psychology, the **fundamental attribution error** (also known as **correspondence bias** or **attribution effect**) describes the tendency to over-value dispositional or personality-based explanations for the observed behaviours of others while under-valuing situational explanations for those behaviors. The fundamental attribution error is most visible when people explain the behavior of others. It does not explain interpretations of one's own behaviour – where situational factors are often taken into consideration. This discrepancy is called the actor–observer bias.

As a simple example, consider a situation where a driver, Alice, is about to pass through an intersection. Her light turns green, and so she begins moving forward when an ambulance blows through the red-light with sirens blaring and lights flashing, and cuts her off. Despite knowing that there is a good reason for the driver's behavior, she is likely to form a negative opinion of the driver, e.g. "what an inconsiderate driver!"'

Source: Wikipedia. Fundamental attribution error. Retrieved January 4, 2013, from http://en.wikipedia.org/wiki/Fundamental_attribution_error. Used under the Creative Commons License http://creativecommons.org/licenses/by-sa/3.0/.

If you find some concepts particularly difficult remind yourself why the concepts may be useful or interesting. If you need to refer to it in your essay, but it does not appeal to you, find out why others find it interesting. This will give you the motivation to make the necessary effort to explore it further.

Tips

Being more active as you are reading can also help you work through complex ideas. Try:

✓ pausing after each section to summarize the text in your own words
✓ representing the information in a diagram
✓ making notes.

For more on active reading skills, see Chapter 6 and for more on note making, see Chapter 8.

Strategies for dealing with long and complex sentences

Glossary

complex sentence
A complex sentence contains one or more subordinate clauses as well as a main clause.

main clause
The main clause in a complex sentence is the group of words that contains at least a subject and a verb, and can stand alone as a complete sentence.

line of reasoning
In a text, the line of reasoning is the way in which the author's thoughts and argument develop.

If you find yourself getting lost in long and complex sentences, or if you find you cannot make sense of a sentence even though you are familiar with all of the words in it, try breaking the sentence down into parts. Often the main idea of a sentence will be expressed in the main clause. To find the main clause, ignore phrases that begin with prepositions such as 'in', 'for' or 'about' and clauses that begin with subordinators such as 'when', 'since' or 'as'. Highlight the main subject, verb and object (if present) in each sentence of the passage. Read the words that you have highlighted until you have a rough idea of content. Then read the passage in full focussing on how the main points are modified and connected. If it helps you, make a diagram to represent the author's line of reasoning.

> **For example, you might highlight the sentence below from the text in Exercise 2 in the following way:**
>
> Social exchange theory is, in a sense, a member of the general family of behaviourist theories, but as an approach to studying interpersonal relationships it also incorporates *interaction*.
>
> The highlighted parts put together make a more manageable sentence:
>
> 'Social exchange theory is behaviourist but also incorporates interaction.'

Exercise 7

Look again at the passage in Exercise 4. How difficult is it for you now? Then, locate a difficult passage (100 – 200 words long) in your own reading and follow steps 1–5 below.

1   Identify the unfamiliar vocabulary and check the definitions of those words that appear to be important.

2   'Translate' the topic sentence and concluding sentence into your own words.

3   If there are unfamiliar concepts in the passage, explore them further in an online (or print) encyclopaedia.

4   Highlight the main clause of each sentence.

5   Make notes or draw a diagram to represent the main ideas in the passage.

Which of the strategies above did you find most helpful?

Remember

✔   Use fast reading strategies to manage large amounts of information.

✔   Skim texts to assess the relevance and identify the main points: read the first and last paragraphs in full, read the first line or sentence of all the other paragraphs.

✔   If the first sentence in a paragraph does not appear to express the main point, look at the second and last sentences in the paragraph.

✔   To scan for specific information, skim the text first to identify the part of the text most likely to contain what you are looking for.

✔   To make sense of a difficult passage, study the definitions of key words, particularly those that occur in the topic and concluding sentences.

✔   When dealing with unfamiliar concepts, know when to get more background information and make more use of active reading strategies.

✔   Work out the meaning of complex sentences by identifying the main clause. Do this for each sentence in a difficult passage; then re-read the passage focusing on how the main ideas are connected.

6 | Reading more efficiently

Aims ✓ improve your concentration when reading
✓ guess the meaning of unfamiliar words from context

✓ improve your reading speed

Aims

? Quiz
Self-evaluation

Read the statements, then circle the word which is true for you.

1	I usually begin reading without any particular ideas about the topic.	agree | disagree | not sure
2	I usually read every word of the text from start to finish.	agree | disagree | not sure
3	I frequently lose concentration when I'm reading.	agree | disagree | not sure
4	I feel guilty if I don't look up unfamiliar vocabulary in the dictionary.	agree | disagree | not sure
5	I often have no clear opinion about what I am reading.	agree | disagree | not sure

Being an active reader

It is important to find ways of reading more efficiently in order to handle both the volume and depth of information involved in doing research. Learning to manage yourself as a reader is just as important as learning to manage reading texts. This means taking steps to help yourself actively engage with new information and ideas. In the previous chapter, we looked at a range of reading strategies that can be used for different purposes. Here, we will look at techniques that you can use to increase your reading speed and improve your concentration whatever your reason for reading.

Preparing to read

Whether you are skimming a text or reading intensively, it is important to prepare your mind so that you are as receptive as possible to new information. New information is generally easier to absorb if it has something to connect to. This might be prior knowledge about the topic, or questions that you would like answered. It is therefore useful to spend a little time bringing to mind what you have learned about the topic, either from personal experience or through your reading. Focus on what you have found most interesting and relevant to your essay question.

Then focus on stimulating your curiosity. Think about what you would most like to learn from the reading text in front of you. Frame questions in your mind, or write them down. You do not necessarily need to keep your questions in mind as you are reading. Simply framing questions is often enough to get you reading more actively.

Exercise 1

Imagine that you are writing an essay about the effect of social media use on young people and that you have found the article below.

Think about what you already know about Facebook, either from your personal experience or from reading or hearing about it. Write three questions that you would like the text to answer.

Then read the abstract and see if you can find answers to your questions.

Facebook, as one of the most popular social networking sites among college students, provides a platform for people to manage others' impressions of them. People tend to present themselves in a favorable way on their Facebook profile. This research examines the impact of using Facebook on people's perceptions of others' lives. It is argued that those with deeper involvement with Facebook will have different perceptions of others than those less involved due to two reasons. First, Facebook users tend to base judgment on examples easily recalled […]. Second, Facebook users tend to attribute the positive content presented on Facebook to others' personality, rather than situational factors 29–32 (correspondence bias), especially for those they do not know personally. Questionnaires, including items measuring years of using Facebook, time spent on Facebook each week, number of people listed as their Facebook "friends", and perceptions about others' lives, were completed by 425 undergraduate students taking classes across various academic disciplines at a state university in Utah. Surveys were collected during regular class period, except for two online classes where surveys were submitted online. The multivariate analysis indicated that those who have used Facebook longer agreed more that others were happier, and agreed less that life is fair, and those spending more time on Facebook each week agreed more that others were happier and had better lives. Furthermore, those that included more people whom they did not personally know as their Facebook "friends" agreed more that others had better lives.

Source: Chou, H. G., & Edge, N. (2012). "They Are Happier and Having Better Lives than I Am": The Impact of Using Facebook on Perceptions of Others' Lives. *Cyberpsychology, Behavior, and Social Networking, 15(2),* 117–121.

It does not matter if some of your questions are not answered. In terms of reading efficiency, having a questioning mind is what makes you more receptive to the information – even information that you didn't expect to find.

Using questions to maintain concentration

Glossary

anticipate
If you anticipate an event, you realize in advance that it may happen and you are prepared for it.

Efficient readers ask questions not only before but also while reading a text. This allows them to anticipate what is coming and maintain concentration. The extract below comes from the introduction to the article. Notice the questions in brackets that you might ask yourself while reading the text.

For example:

When making judgments or forming impressions about others, one common attribution error is the correspondence bias *[WHAT IS 'CORRESPONDENCE BIAS'?]* ; that is, the tendency to assume that others' actions and words reflect their personality or stable personal disposition, rather than being affected by situational factors 29–32 *[HOW DOES THIS RELATE TO FACEBOOK USE?]* When seeing others' happy pictures posted on Facebook, users might conclude that others are happy, while ignoring the circumstances or situations that made others happy. The correspondence bias is more likely to happen when Facebook users make attributions about people whom they have never met before. *[WHY?]* They assume that happiness is a stable characteristic of their temperaments and that they are constantly enjoying good lives. For those they do know personally, however, their past interactions with them help Facebook users avoid the trap of correspondence bias and recognize the external factors at work: it is the occasions that make their friends happy.

Source: Chou, H. G. & Edge, N. (2012). "They Are Happier and Having Better Lives than I Am": The Impact of Using Facebook on Perceptions of Others' Lives. *Cyberpsychology, Behavior, and Social Networking, 15(2)*, 117–121.

Some questions may be answered in the very next sentence, whereas others may be answered later or not at all. Again, remember that the purpose of framing questions is to stimulate your curiosity and maintain concentration.

Tips   When framing questions for reading, use:

- ✓ 'What' questions for key concepts (e.g. What is 'correspondence bias'?)
- ✓ 'How' questions for processes and methods (e.g. How does correspondence bias relate to Facebook use? How did the researchers investigate this phenomenon?)
- ✓ 'Why' questions for reasons (e.g. Why is correspondence bias more likely to happen when Facebook users make attributions about people whom they have never met before?)
- ✓ 'So what' questions for significance (e.g. So what is the significance of these findings?)

Exercise 2

Read the abstract below. In the brackets, write questions that you might ask yourself while reading.

The social network site Facebook is a rapidly expanding phenomenon that is changing the nature of social relationships. [1 ...   ] Anecdotal evidence, including information described in the popular media, suggests that Facebook may be responsible for creating jealousy and suspicion in romantic relationships. [2 ...   ] The objectives of the present study were to explore the role of Facebook in the experience of jealousy and to determine if increased Facebook exposure predicts jealousy above and beyond personal and relationship factors. [3 ...   ] Three hundred eight undergraduate students completed an online survey that assessed demographic and personality factors and explored respondents' Facebook use. A hierarchical multiple regression analysis [4 ...   ], controlling for individual, personality, and relationship factors, revealed that increased Facebook use significantly predicts Facebook-related jealousy. [5 ...   ] We argue that this effect may be the result of a feedback loop whereby using Facebook exposes people to often ambiguous information about their partner that they may not otherwise have access to and that this new information incites further Facebook use. [6 ...   ] Our study provides evidence of Facebook's unique contributions to the experience of jealousy in romantic relationships.

Source: Extract from Muise, A., Christofides, E., & Desmarais, S. (2009). More Information than You Ever Wanted: Does Facebook Bring Out the Green-Eyed Monster of Jealousy? *CyberPsychology & Behavior*, 12(4), 441–444.

Tips Asking questions of the text is not the only way of maintaining concentration. Other techniques you can use include:

- ✓ summarizing the text in your own words as you read
- ✓ comparing what you are reading to your prior knowledge
- ✓ pausing to form an opinion of what you are reading
- ✓ underlining, highlighting or annotating the text
- ✓ making notes.

Any activity that keeps you personally engaged with the text will help you maintain concentration.

For more on annotating, see Chapter 4. For more on note making, see Chapter 8.

Using the dictionary selectively

Glossary

obstacle
An obstacle is anything that makes it difficult for you to do something.

The need to deal with unfamiliar vocabulary can be a major obstacle to efficient reading. Some learners feel guilty if they do not check every new word in the dictionary. In fact, efficient readers are very selective about which words they look up. In most cases, only checking those words that are crucial for understanding the main point allows you to maintain your concentration.

Tips Be selective about which words you check in the dictionary. Give priority to words that appear:

✓ in the title
✓ in headings and subheadings
✓ in topic sentences
✓ around signposting expressions of significance (e.g. 'however', 'main', 'significant')
✓ repeatedly throughout the passage.

Exercise 3

Read the extract below which comes from the results section of the article and underline the words that you do not know. Circle the words that you would look up in a dictionary.

Our results suggest that Facebook may expose an individual to potentially jealousy-provoking information about their partner, which creates a feedback loop whereby heightened jealousy leads to increased surveillance of a partner's Facebook page. Persistent surveillance results in further exposure to jealousy-provoking information. For many, the need for knowledge about their partner's intent becomes indispensable, and several participants specifically mentioned the word "addiction" in relation to their own Facebook usage. One participant who had recently broken up with her boyfriend stated, "It's addictive....I always find myself going on there checking new pictures and screening them. I can't help it!" Our finding of a link between jealousy triggers on Facebook and increased surveillance of a partner's profile has also been discussed in some popular media,[4] suggesting that this phenomenon is not limited to the current sample. However, our study is the first to test this hypothesis and to control for personality and social factors that may have confounded the results.

Source: Extract from Muise, A., Christofides, E., & Desmarais, S. (2009). More Information than You Ever Wanted: Does Facebook Bring Out the Green-Eyed Monster of Jealousy? *CyberPsychology & Behavior, 12(4)*, 441–444.

Guessing the meaning of vocabulary from context

Glossary

gregarious
Someone who is gregarious enjoys being with other people.

paraphrase
A paraphrase of something written or spoken is the same thing expressed in a different way.

deduce
If you deduce something you reach that conclusion because of other things that you know to be true.

In many cases, you can guess the meaning of an unfamiliar word from the context. To do this, you need to establish the relationship between the unfamiliar word and the other words around it. Begin by identifying the 'part of speech', that is, whether the word is a noun, verb, adjective, adverb or conjunction. You can do this by looking at words that immediately precede or follow the word. For example, if the word you do not know lies between an article ('a', 'an', or 'the') and a noun, it is likely to be an adjective (for example, the adjective 'gregarious' might appear in phrases such as 'the **gregarious** children'). Certain word endings can also help you recognize part of speech. For example, '-tion', '-ism' and '-ship' denote nouns, whereas '-al', '-ile' and '-ic' frequently appear at the end of adjectives.

Then ask yourself:

- Is the unfamiliar word a synonym or paraphrase of another word in the text?

- Is it an example?

- Is it a general term that refers to items in a list?

- Is it contrasted with another word in the text?

- Is it a cause or effect?

For example, notice the word '*kale*' in the sentence below:

*This delicious vegetable soup contains carrots, onions, **kale** and tomatoes.*

You can deduce that the word 'kale' is a noun because it is the object of the verb 'contain' and occurs in a list of other nouns. You can also make a reasonable assumption that it is a type of vegetable because of the name of the dish.

Try not to worry too much about guessing incorrectly. Often an inexact or incorrect guess does not matter if the information is not crucial for understanding the main point. In the example above, if you guessed that kale was a kind of spice rather than a vegetable, it probably would not matter unless you were planning to cook or eat the soup! Moreover, if you do guess incorrectly and the information is important, you will usually soon discover this when you read on and the passage stops making sense. You can always go back and check the word in your dictionary at that point.

Exercise 4

Use the context to work out the part of speech of each word in bold in sentences 1–5. Indicate whether the word is a synonym, example, general term, contrasting term, cause or effect. Try to guess the meaning of the word, then check the definition in the answer key.

1 Some students **eagerly** awaited their test results, whereas others appeared unconcerned.

2 Personality **traits**, such as openness, warmth and kindness, were highly rated by the participants.

3 The professor's **charisma** inspired great loyalty among his students.

4 We do not generally trust people who seek out **clandestine** relationships. Moreover, this type of secretive relationship is rarely good for the people involved.

5 Experiencing frequent criticism in childhood can result in a tendency towards **inhibition**.

Recognizing parts of words

Glossary

prefix
A prefix is a letter or a group of letters, for example 'un-' or 'multi-', which is added to the beginning of a word in order to form a different word.

suffix
A suffix is a letter or a group of letters, for example '-ly' or '-ness', which is added to the end of a word in order to form a different word, often of a different word class.

You can also sometimes work out the meaning of an unfamiliar word by analysing the word itself. This involves looking for prefixes, suffixes and the root or main part of the word. Common prefixes include: anti- (meaning 'against'), mono- (meaning 'one') and post- (meaning 'after'). Common suffixes include -ful (meaning 'with') and -less (meaning 'without').

See the Appendix for a list of common prefixes and suffixes.

Once you have identified the main part of the word, you may be able to guess its meaning if you recognize similarities to other words that you know.

For example, you may have noticed the expression 'multivariate analysis' in the abstract you read for Exercise 1. This looks like a difficult term, but if you break the word 'multivariate' down into parts, you will see that it consists of:

- the prefix 'multi' meaning two or more

- the main part 'vari' meaning changeable or diverse (you might recognize it in the words 'vary', 'variety' or 'variable')

- the word ending 'ate' which often indicates the word is an adjective.

The expression 'multivariate analysis' thus means: analysis of two or more things that change.

Recognizing similarities among words will help you learn common prefixes, suffixes and roots. For example, if you know that *careless* means 'without care' and *worthless* means 'without worth or value', you can work out that the suffix *-less* means 'without'.

Exercise 5

Study the definitions of the word pairs 1–5 to work out the meaning of the prefix, suffix or root in italics.

1 a *ambi*dextrous – (adj) Someone who is ambidextrous can use both their right hand and their left hand equally skilfully.
   b *ambi*guous – (adj) If you describe something as ambiguous, you mean that it is unclear or confusing because it can be understood in more than one way.
      ambi- means _____

2 a *ante*cedent – (n) An antecedent of something happened or existed before it and was similar to it in some way.
   b *ante*room – (n) An anteroom is a small room leading into a larger room.
      ante- means _____

3 a as*cert*ain – (v) If you ascertain the truth about something, you find out what it is, especially by making a deliberate effort to do so.
   b *cert*ificate – (n) A certificate is an official document stating that particular facts are true.
      cert- means _____

4 a *hyper*active – (adj) Someone who is hyperactive is unable to relax and is always moving about or doing things.
   b *hyper*sensitive – (adj) If you say that someone is hypersensitive, you mean they get annoyed or offended very easily.
      hyper- means _____

5 a fals*ify* – (v) If someone falsifies something, they change it or add untrue details to it in order to deceive people.
   b magn*ify* – (v) To magnify an object means to make it appear larger than it really is, by means of a special lens or mirror.
      -ify means _____

Exercise 6

Work out the meanings of words 1–10 below by breaking them down into parts. Then check the answer key.

1	anticlockwise	4	monotheism	7	semi-detached	9	contradict
2	disclosure	5	deforestation	8	bilingual	10	precondition
3	unforeseen	6	uniformity				

Exercise 7

Look again at the words you underlined in Exercise 3 and try to guess the meaning. Use your dictionary to check if your guess was correct or close enough to get the main idea.

Reading sentences in 'chunks'

If you read actively, and regularly guess the meaning of unfamiliar words, but you still find that your reading is very slow, you may benefit from looking more carefully at how you move your eyes across the text. One common reason for slow reading is the tendency to focus on words individually rather than on groups of words or 'chunks'.

Exercise 8

Read the sentence below from the abstract in Exercise 2 by covering it with a slip of paper and revealing the sentence word by word.

The   social   networking   site   Facebook   is   a   rapidly   expanding   phenomenon   that   is   changing   the   nature   of   social   relationships.

Now read the same sentence in chunks.

The social networking site Facebook   is a rapidly expanding phenomenon   that is changing the nature   of social relationships.

Reading a text word by word is slow because the eye stops frequently (18 times versus five times in the example above). It can also result in poorer comprehension because meaning is often carried by groups of words rather than by individual words.

How exactly you divide sentences into chunks is not so important – there is no single best way of doing it. Generally chunks from two to five words long are easiest to process, particularly if they are based loosely on noun phrases ('the social networking site'), verb phrases ('is changing') and prepositional phrases ('of social relationships'). The important thing is that you focus on groups of words that make sense to you.

Exercise 9

Indicate with a vertical line how you would break the sentence below into chunks. Then practise reading other sentences from the extract in Exercise 3 chunk by chunk.

> For many, the need for knowledge about their partner's intent becomes indispensable, and several participants specifically mentioned the word "addiction" in relation to their own Facebook usage.

Subvocalizing

Glossary

subvocalize
If you subvocalize when you are reading a text, you move your mouth as if you are speaking the words.

People who read one word at a time, also often subvocalize. This is another common reason for slow reading as it is normally faster to read a text than to speak it.

Reading in chunks can help reduce the tendency to vocalize. However if you have this habit and it persists, it can be helpful to place your hand lightly over your mouth when reading.

Back tracking and how to avoid it

Glossary

reflect on
When you reflect on something, you think deeply about it.

Another common reason for slow reading speeds is 'back tracking', that is the tendency to re-read earlier parts of the sentence or passage before you get to the end. For example the sentence you looked at earlier might be read:

> *The social networking site social networking site Facebook is a rapidly expanding Facebook is a rapidly expanding phenomenon that is changing the nature of social changing the nature of social relationships.*

If you have a tendency to back track, train yourself to read more efficiently by moving your finger forward along the text as you read until you reach a full stop. Then reflect on what you have understood. If you cannot summarize the main point of the sentence in your own way, you can re-read it from start to finish.

Exercise 10

Read abstracts 1 and 2 below using the techniques described in this chapter – see the 'Remember' section at the end of the chapter to remind yourself of what these are.

1   College students' social networking experiences on Facebook

Millions of contemporary young adults use social networking sites. However, little is known about how much, why, and how they use these sites. In this study, 92 undergraduates completed a diary-like measure each day for a week, reporting daily time use and responding to an activities checklist to assess their use of the popular social networking site, Facebook. At the end of the week, they also completed a follow-up survey. Results indicated that students use Facebook approximately 30 min throughout the day as part of their daily routine. Students communicated on Facebook using a one-to-many style, in which they were the creators disseminating content to their friends. Even so, they spent more time observing content on Facebook than actually posting content. Facebook was used most often for social interaction, primarily with friends with whom the students had a pre-established relationship offline. In addition to classic identity markers of emerging adulthood, such as religion, political ideology, and work, young adults also used media preferences to express their identity. Implications of social networking site use for the development of identity and peer relationships are discussed.

Source: Extract from College students' social networking experiences on Facebook by Pempek, T. A., Yermolayeva, Y. A.. & Calvert, S. L. (2009). *Journal of Applied Developmental Psychology*, 30 (3), 227–238.

2   Actually, I Wanted to Learn

Social media open up multiple options to add a new dimension to learning and knowledge processes. Particularly, social networking sites allow students to connect formal and informal learning settings. Students can find like-minded people and organize informal knowledge exchange for educational purposes. However, little is known about in which way students use social networking sites for informal learning and about characteristics of these students. In this paper, three studies examined the study-related knowledge exchange via StudiVZ, the German equivalent of Facebook. Results indicated that about one fifth of participants exchange study-related knowledge through StudiVZ and that these students are especially freshers seeking contact with other students and orientation. Consistent with previous research, it is shown that students use social networking sites mainly for social interaction and integration. However, results also imply that communication about social issues on social networking sites goes hand in hand with study-related knowledge exchange.

Source: Extract from 'Actually, I wanted to Learn:' Study-related knowledge exchange on social networking sites by Wodzicki, K., Schwämmlein, E., & Moskaliuk, J. (2012) from *The Internet and Higher Education*, 15(1), 9–14.

Remember

✓ Prepare to read by thinking about what you already know about the topic.

✓ Before reading, frame questions to stimulate your curiosity and establish your focus.

✓ Frame questions as you are reading to anticipate what's coming and keep concentration.

✓ Try other techniques for keeping concentration, such as annotating the text or summarizing the main points as you go.

✓ Be selective about which words you look up in the dictionary – focus on key words.

✓ Where possible, work out the meaning of unfamiliar words from context – think about their function in the sentence.

✓ Learn to recognize parts of speech.

✓ Learn to recognize common prefixes and suffixes and similarities between words with common roots.

✓ Read sentences in chunks.

✓ Avoid back tracking by training your eyes to move forward.

7 | Reading critically

Aims ✓ define critical thinking in your study
context
✓ distinguish fact from opinion

✓ reflect critically on your own views
✓ critically evaluate reading texts

Aims

Quiz
Self-evaluation

In your previous experience of study, how acceptable was it for you to do the following? Rate each item from 1 to 4, with 1 = not acceptable, 2 = sometimes acceptable, 3 = usually acceptable and 4 = always acceptable.

1	Express your personal opinion.	
2	Ask questions that do not have straightforward answers.	
3	Openly discuss differences of opinion.	
4	Challenge other students if you felt they were wrong.	
5	Challenge your teachers if you felt they were wrong.	
6	Make judgements about what you read in textbooks.	

What is critical thinking?

Glossary

knowledge claim
A knowledge claim is a statement of what you believe to be true.

Critical thinking skills are often said to be very important in higher education, but what do people mean by critical thinking? Generally, in academic contexts, critical thinking means making judgements about knowledge claims, in other words, making informed decisions about whether statements are valid, partly valid, or invalid. This can be one of the most challenging aspects of higher education, particularly if you have not been previously encouraged to take part in critical debate.

Glossary

Glossary

debate
A debate is a discussion about a subject on which people have different views.

All academic disciplines develop through the process of critically evaluating knowledge claims. However, what this means for you as a student can vary, depending on your subject discipline and stage of learning. Within the natural sciences, for example, students are not generally expected to challenge expert opinion until they have a substantial knowledge base of their own. For undergraduates in these disciplines, 'critical thinking' often means recognizing when they have got information wrong or thinking about how to apply knowledge to solve problems. Students in the social sciences and humanities, on the other hand, are normally expected to demonstrate critical thinking skills right from the start, that is, express their opinions about what they read, hear and discuss.

Whatever your discipline, it is important to remember that it is your *informed* opinions that count. This means that any judgements you make should be based on a thorough and thoughtful investigation of the topic. When you do research, most of your investigation will be done by reading. It is therefore essential to develop good critical reading skills.

Facts versus opinions

Glossary

distinguish
If you can distinguish one thing from another or distinguish between two things, you can see or understand how they are different.

linguist
A linguist is a person who studies how language works.

How you judge a knowledge claim in a reading text depends partly on whether the claim is presented as a fact or an opinion. Some claims are clearly presented as facts, with expressions such as: *We know that ..., X has been shown to be ..., It has been verified that ..., clearly ...,* and *no doubt.* Expressions indicating an opinion include: *In our view ..., X is believed to be ..., The evidence suggests that ..., may, possibly,* and *likely.* However, simply presenting a statement as a fact or as an opinion does not make it necessarily one. You need to have some means of distinguishing fact from opinion for yourself.

This can be difficult to do. Sometimes, a statement can be considered a fact in one context but an opinion in another. For example, in everyday contexts it may be acceptable to make the statement *English is a world language* as a fact; however, linguists might consider the concept of 'world language' a debatable matter of opinion.

Research

Glossary

verifiable
Something that is verifiable can be proved to be true or genuine.

In practice, it may be more helpful to see *facts* as claims that are widely accepted by scholars in your field and easily verifiable, and *opinions* as claims that are more debatable. As you become more familiar with your subject, you will gradually learn what counts as a fact and what counts as an opinion.

Tips As a general rule, it is good to be cautious about claims which are presented as facts but which:

✓ are expressed with force or certainty
✓ are based on imprecise or poorly defined terms
✓ express cause and effect relationships, especially in relation to complex phenomena
✓ involve predictions about the future
✓ make value judgements.

Tips

These are likely to be opinions and not facts because they cannot be easily verified.

Exercise 1

Read statements 1–10. What is the problem with each one?

1 The fact is, computers are simply too expensive.

2 John F. Kennedy is known to have been a good leader.

3 The economic downturn will no doubt persist for a further three years.

4 It has been proven that lack of opportunity for outdoor play leads to depression in children.

5 We know that all people feel envious at times.

6 Of course, the banking crisis was caused by excessive greed and inadequate regulation.

7 In fact, women have always been less ambitious than men.

8 Local residents are unhappy about the visitors' immoral behaviour.

9 The Louvre in Paris is, without a doubt, the world's finest museum.

10 The United Kingdom will never become a republic.

Reflecting critically on your own views

Glossary

position
Your position on a particular matter is your attitude towards it or your opinion of it.

assumption
If you make an assumption that something is true or will happen, you accept that it is true or will happen, often without any real proof.

Reading critically is an intellectually demanding task. As discussed in Chapter 6, you are more likely to read efficiently if you are prepared. This is particularly true if your aim is to make judgements about what you are reading.

A good preparatory exercise is to reflect on your 'uninformed' opinion in relation to your essay question. Ask yourself:

1   What is my 'position' on the question?

2   What are my reasons for holding this opinion?

3   On what evidence have I based my reasoning?

4   What assumptions have I made?

Exercise 2

Consider your views in relation to the essay question presented in Chapter 1: *Is generosity an innate human trait?* Ask yourself questions 1–4 above and note your answers.

Once you have clarified your views, you can begin to think more critically about them by asking yourself further questions.

For example:

Imagine your have responded to Exercise 2 in the following way:

Your position: Generosity is not innate.

Your reason: People learn to be generous.

Your evidence: You remember being taught to be generous by your parents and teachers.

Your assumptions: Generosity means doing something for another person without expecting a reward. Generosity does in fact exist, and people are generous at least some of the time.

You can then ask yourself:

1   Are my assumptions in fact true?

If you think carefully about your experience, you may recall receiving rewards for your generous behaviour, approval from your parents, for example. Is it possible that people are always motivated by a desire for reward? Is it possible that generosity does not in fact exist? Do you need to investigate the concept of generosity further?

2   How solid is my evidence?

You may remember learning to be generous, but how *representative* are you of human beings generally? Do you need a larger *sample* of people from which to draw your conclusions? How *reliable* is your memory? Have you ignored evidence that would support other points of view?

3   How sound is my reasoning?

Even if your evidence is good, should you conclude that generosity is only learned? Is it possible that people have an innate tendency to learn and teach others to behave generously?

4   Is it possible that my position is biased in some way?

Could your needs and desires influence your reasoning more than you think? Could your opinion be based, for example, on a need to believe that people are kind and that learning is important?

This process of self-reflection should open your mind to considering the research question from alternative points of view.

Tips   Before taking a critical view of a text:
   ✓   Clarify your views on the topic.
   ✓   Be prepared to read with an open mind.
   ✓   Allow yourself to change your opinion – perhaps several times – as you explore your topic more deeply.

Exercise 3

Look at your own responses to Exercise 2 and ask yourself questions 1–4 above. How comfortable do you feel about critically examining your own thinking?

Make a plan for reading

Systematically questioning your own views in this way, will give you a clearer idea of how to approach your reading. Using the example on the previous page, you might decide that you need to look for texts that will help you:

- define key terms, for example 'generosity' ■ verify your opinion by supplying you with additional reasons and evidence ■ explore alternative arguments and evidence.

A good place to start looking for this information is an up-to-date textbook that covers the topic. Textbooks will often help you define key terms and understand the main concepts. They also give an overview of the research area and summarize the key studies that have shaped the debate. This overview can be a very helpful starting point for further exploration. It gives you a context from which to understand and critically evaluate other books and articles on the topic.

Tips When using a textbook for research:

✓ Use the table of contents to locate the relevant chapter(s).
✓ Read first for a general understanding of the key terms and concepts.
✓ Re-read carefully any section describing the research area and note the key studies mentioned.
✓ Use this information to guide your further reading.

For more information on finding source texts, see Chapter 2.

Exercise 4

The extract below comes from a psychology textbook and deals with the topic of helping behaviour. Read the extract and answer questions 1 and 2.

1   How do the authors define the research area?

2   Which of these areas would you explore further in order to answer the question: *Is generosity an innate human trait?*

'The question of why people help others is obviously an important one. We address two major viewpoints in the following sections, one grounded in evolutionary theory and the other in social learning theory. This distinction is significant and represents important differences among psychologists generally, as well as among some social psychologists. Other views give a more biosocial account, reflecting the role of empathy, cognition, and characteristics of the situation in which help is either given or not.'

Source: Extracts from Vaughan & Hogg, Psychology © 2011 Pearson Australia pp 544–545, 537–538, 498.

Identifying the arguments within reading texts

It is helpful to begin reading with an open mind. Once you have a good understanding of the text on its own terms, you can then apply the same approach that you use to critically examine your own thinking.

The first stage is to clarify the main components of the argument: the author's position, reasoning, evidence and assumptions, like you did for your own views in preparation for Exercise 2.

Exercise 5

Read the text below which summarizes a well-known experiment investigating helping behaviour. Answer questions 1–4.

1   What do you think the experimenters' **position** might be on the question of whether or not generosity is innate?

2   What **reason or reasons** might they give?

3   What **evidence** could they offer to support their view?

4   What **assumptions** do you think they have made?

'Working from a social learning perspective, Bryan and Test (1967) devised the following experiment. In one condition, motorists witnessed a model of helping behaviour staged by the experimenters: a woman motorist stranded by the side of the road was receiving assistance from a man. In another condition, motorists were presented with a woman stranded by the side of the road, but this time receiving no assistance. For both conditions, the experimenters placed another woman motorist several hundred metres further down the road who clearly required help with a punctured tyre. Bryan and Test found that of the 4000 passing cars, 50% more drivers stopped to assist the woman requiring help if they had passed the model helper.'

Sometimes it is easy to identify the components of the author's argument. The author's position, for example, may be signposted with expressions such as: 'we conclude that …', 'it is our belief that …', 'in our view …'. The author's reasoning and evidence may also be signalled by words such as: 'because', 'since', 'as', and 'given that'. However, in many instances, you need to infer these elements.

Exercise 6

Look again at one of the abstracts about social media use that you studied earlier. Label the sections of the abstract that best summarize the authors' position, reasoning, evidence, and assumptions. Then, underline any signpost expressions that help you identify these elements.

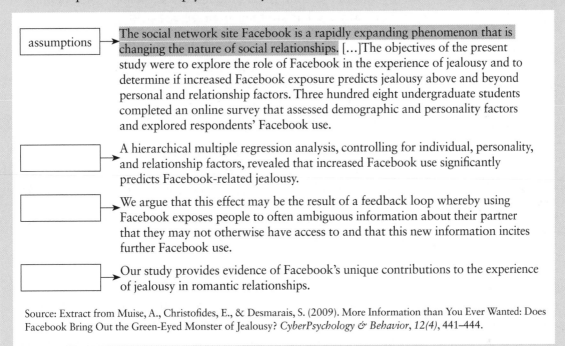

assumptions → The social network site Facebook is a rapidly expanding phenomenon that is changing the nature of social relationships. [...]The objectives of the present study were to explore the role of Facebook in the experience of jealousy and to determine if increased Facebook exposure predicts jealousy above and beyond personal and relationship factors. Three hundred eight undergraduate students completed an online survey that assessed demographic and personality factors and explored respondents' Facebook use.

→ A hierarchical multiple regression analysis, controlling for individual, personality, and relationship factors, revealed that increased Facebook use significantly predicts Facebook-related jealousy.

→ We argue that this effect may be the result of a feedback loop whereby using Facebook exposes people to often ambiguous information about their partner that they may not otherwise have access to and that this new information incites further Facebook use.

→ Our study provides evidence of Facebook's unique contributions to the experience of jealousy in romantic relationships.

Source: Extract from Muise, A., Christofides, E., & Desmarais, S. (2009). More Information than You Ever Wanted: Does Facebook Bring Out the Green-Eyed Monster of Jealousy? *CyberPsychology & Behavior, 12(4)*, 441–444.

Thinking critically about the arguments within texts

Once you have identified the argument within the text, you can then apply the same questions that you ask yourself when critically challenging your own thinking.

1   Are the authors' assumptions in fact true? How have they defined their key terms? What are their premises?

2   How solid is the evidence presented? Are examples given? If the evidence is statistical, how large and how representative is the sample? Have the authors used reliable methods to gather and analyse the data? Have the authors ignored evidence that would support other points of view? If so, how good is that other evidence?

3   How sound is the authors' reasoning? Would it be possible to interpret their evidence in a different way and arrive at a different conclusion? Could there be any other reasons for what happened?

4   In what ways might the authors be biased? Do they have a vested interest in seeing the issue in a certain way?

Answering questions of this type can be difficult. You often need to use your knowledge of the research area and other studies to support the judgements that you make. It is therefore important to read widely and then think about how one study might relate to another. Generally speaking, the more you have explored the issue, the easier it will be for you to think critically about what you read.

Exercise 7

Look again at your responses to Exercise 5. Which of the questions above can you answer?

Exercise 8

Read the commentary below and compare it to your answers in Exercise 7.

'The study appears to support the view that generosity is learned from models. The sample is large and the results are statistically significant. However, because the researchers have based their findings on observed behaviour rather than on interviews, we do not really know about the motives of those who stopped to help. A number of studies, most notably, Pszybyla (1985), have found that men are significantly more likely to help a woman than another man, and that they are often more likely to do so when they feel there is the possibility of a romantic encounter. It is therefore difficult to conclude with any certainty that the motorists observed by Bryan and Test were motivated by a desire to be helpful and not for other more self-interested reasons. The choice of location for the study may have introduced a further confounding variable. Amato (1983), investigating the relationship between population size and helping behaviour, found that people who lived in small communities were significantly more likely to help a stranger than people from large cities. If Bryan and Test did not place both conditions along the same stretch of road, some of the variation in behaviour that they observed may have been due to the choice of location.'

For a more extensive list of questions to ask yourself when evaluating source material, see Appendix 1.

Remember

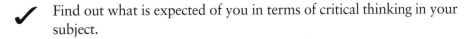

✓   Find out what is expected of you in terms of critical thinking in your subject.

✓   Learn to distinguish between facts and opinions.

✓   Read textbooks to learn about the research territory around your essay question.

✓   Read books and articles that both support and challenge your position.

✓   Be prepared to change your mind.

✓   Learn to recognize the key features of arguments: position, reasons, evidence, premises.

✓   Question these features systematically.

✓   Read widely to ensure that your opinions of any given text are informed by your knowledge of other texts.

8 | Making notes

Quiz
Self-evaluation

When gathering information for an essay, how often do you do the following? (Rate each item from 1 to 4 with 1 = never, 2 = sometimes, 3 = often and 4 = always.)

1	Highlight or annotate reading texts	
2	Write notes as a list or outline	
3	Make notes in a diagram form	
4	Copy and paste information directly from the web into your essay	
5	Note the bibliographic details of your source texts	

Knowing when, why and how to make notes

Making notes can be time consuming and labour intensive. However, if you are using a large number of sources, it is much easier to work from notes when it is time to write your essay. When you are making notes from a reading text in order to write an essay, there is no need to note all of the main points in the source text. If you are still at an early exploratory stage of reading, note the bibliographic information and the points that seem particularly relevant and interesting. Keep a copy of the full text if possible, so that if necessary you can go back and expand on your notes.

If you have already worked out your argument in some detail, try using your essay outline as a framework for note making. Note only the information that is relevant. Ideally, at this stage, every time you make a note from a text, you should have a rough idea of where you are going to put the information and how it is going to contribute to your essay.

When making notes, you may want to begin by highlighting the relevant parts of the source text, or, if you are working online, copying and pasting portions of the text into a notes document. However, it is very important to then *rewrite* the information in note form using your own words. Doing this ensures that you understand the information thoroughly. Moreover, if you only highlight and/or annotate texts, it will be more difficult for you to avoid plagiarizing the material when you write up. When noting information in your own words, take care to represent the author's meaning accurately and to record the bibliographic details of the source.

For more information on avoiding plagiarism, see Chapter 12.

Exercise 1

In this chapter, you will be studying notes a student has made for an essay in response to the following instruction:

Critically examine two approaches to the study of leadership within organizations.

Before looking at her notes, think about your own views on leadership, and answer questions 1–5.

1   Why do you think that some people become effective leaders within organizations and others do not?

2   Is it because some people are leaders by nature?

3   If so, what qualities would you expect a 'born' leader to have?

4   Or do you think that certain circumstances create leaders?

5   If so, what might those circumstances be?

Exercise 2

Now read the student's rough outline and notes a–l. Cross out any notes that are irrelevant. Indicate where in the outline you think the remainder of the notes should be placed by writing letters a–l in the appropriate spaces.

Outline

Introduction

c __

1 Traits approach

__ __ __ __ __ __

2 Situational theories

__ __ __

Student's notes:

a   Traits approach = leader's character most important; leaders born not made

b   Tannenbaum & Schmidt (1973) one of 1st to devise situational model

c   Many ways of looking at leadership

d   Lists of traits produced by different studies tend to be overlapping, subjective & contradictory

e   Emphasis of situational theories: situation is important; no single style of leadership suitable for all situations

f   3 types of firms: sole proprietorship, partnership & corporation

g   Difficult to say how particular personal qualities, e.g. charisma, contribute to firm's performance

h   According to Tannenbaum & Schmidt (1973), some situations require 'boss-centred' leadership, others 'subordinate-centred leadership'

i   'self-confidence, initiative, intelligence and belief in one's actions' commonly seen as essential characteristics of effective leaders (Mullins, 2010: 377)

j   Many trait studies done 1904 to 1970; still influential

k   Over 400 definitions of leadership exist! (Crainer, 1995)

l   Some 'good' leaders succeed in one company but fail in others, e.g. Bob Horton of BP

Source: Extracts and table from *Management and Organisational Behaviour* by L J Mullins © 2010.

Noting information word-for-word

Sometimes you may want to note information word-for-word because in your essay you want to quote directly from the source material. Quoting directly is often a good idea when there is something special about the wording of the source material and not just the ideas or information it conveys.

Tips   When noting information word-for-word:

✓   Copy the text exactly.
✓   Use quotation marks around the material.
✓   Retain original features such as italics, underlines and errors.
✓   Note the page number of the extract along with the other bibliographic information.

For more information on when and how to quote word-for-word, see Chapter 12.

Exercise 3

Imagine a student is writing an essay comparing individual and team performance and has made notes from the text below. What mistakes has the student made?

One particular feature of group versus individual performance is the concept of social loafing and the 'Ringelmann effect', which is the tendency for individuals to expend less effort when working as a member of a group than as an individual. A German psychologist, Ringelmann, compared the results of individual and group performance on a rope-pulling task. Workers were asked to pull as hard as they could on a rope, performing the task first individually and then with others in groups of varying size. A meter measured the strength of each pull. Although the total amount of force did increase with the size of the work group, the effort expended by each individual member decreased with the result that the total group effort was less than the expected sum of the individual contributions.[20] Replications of the Ringelmann effect have generally been supportive of the original findings. [21']

Source: Extracts and table from *Management and Organisational Behaviour* by L J Mullins © 2010.

Student's notes:

1   Ringlemann effect = tendency for individuals to expend less effort when working as a member of a group than as an individual (pp. 353-354)

2   Rope-pulling experiment showed 'the total amount of force did increase with the size of the work group, but the effort expended by each individual member decreased'

3   Similar studies have not confirmed these results

Note-making styles

Different note-making styles or formats can be used for different types of information. The most common practice is to make a list of the points you want to record (like the student's notes in Exercise 2). This is fast and easy, but it can be difficult to see the relationships between ideas and to find specific information when you need to incorporate it into your essay. To help you remember the relationships between important ideas, add headings for categories of information and distinguish between main and supporting or less important points.

Tips To show the difference between main and subordinate points, use:

✓ indentation
✓ numbers or letters
✓ bullet points or stars
✓ underlining
✓ colour

Tips

Exercise 4

Using numbers, letters and indentation, rewrite the notes below so that the relationships between the main and subordinate points are clear.

■ Corporations require leaders able to manage large teams & operate strategically

■ Sole trader – most common type of company

■ There are 3 main types of company

■ Different leadership skills needed for different types of enterprises

■ Partnership – 2nd most common

■ Corporation – different from sole trader & partnership; a 'separate legal entity'

Cornell method

In many cases you will want to add your own comments as you make notes. Adding your own comments ensures that you are really thinking about the source material and how it will contribute to your essay. One way to do this is to divide your paper vertically; use one column to record notes from the text and the other to add your own comments on the material. This will help you clearly distinguish your own ideas from those of the author. Moreover, when you are writing your paper, you may find that your comments help you find the information you need.

For example:

Comments:	Source: Mullins, L. J. (2010). Management and Organisational Behaviour. Harlow, Essex: Pearson Education. pp. 373–390.
good opening point for essay (?)	Introduction **a** Many ways of looking at leadership **b** Over 400 definitions of leadership exist! (Crainer, 1995)
main features	**1** Traits approach **a** Traits approach = leader's character most important; leaders born not made
support for traits approach	**b** Many trait studies done 1904 to 1970; still influential
examples of traits	**c** 'self-confidence, initiative, intelligence and belief in one's actions' commonly seen as essential characteristics of effective leaders (Mullins, 2010: 377)
problems with traits approach (find examples for points d & e?)	**d** Lists of traits produced by different studies tend to be overlapping, subjective & contradictory **e** Difficult to say how particular personal qualities, e.g. charisma, contribute to firm's performance **f** some 'good' leaders successful in one situation but fail in others, e.g. Bob Horton of BP

Exercise 5

Add comments to this page of the student's notes.

Your comments	Notes from Mullins, L. J. (2010) continued.
	2 Situational theories
	a Emphasis of situational theories: situation is important; no single style of leadership suitable for all situations
	b Tannenbaum & Schmidt (1973), one of 1st to devise situational model
	c According to Tannenbaum & Schmidt (1973), some situations require 'boss-centred' leadership, others require 'subordinate-centred leadership'

Using tables to make notes

Sometimes it can be useful to make tables to compare and contrast information and to notice patterns in large amounts of information. It can also help you see what information you may be missing.

Exercise 6

Complete as much of the table below as you can using the notes on the previous page. Put a line through any box that you are not able to complete.

Approach	Main features	Examples	Strengths	Problems
Traits	*1 a*			
Situational				

Using diagrams to make notes

Another common way of representing information is to make a diagram or 'mind map'. This allows you to visualize the information and can help you notice patterns and connections.

For example:

The student's notes on leadership could be represented like this:

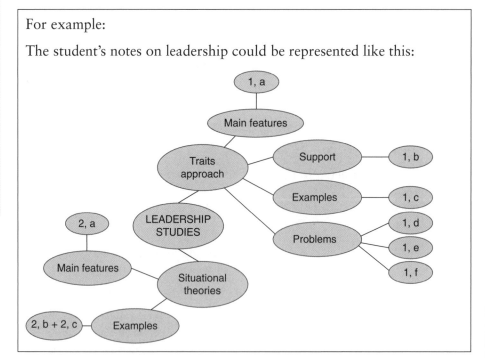

There are many types of diagrams that you can use to represent different types of information.

1 Cause and effect

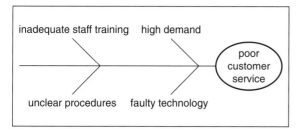

Figure 1: Reasons for poor customer service

2 Process

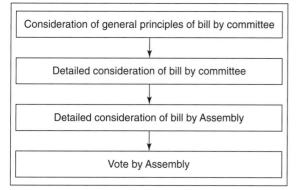

Figure 2: The legislative process

3 Cycle

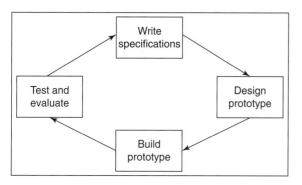

Figure 3: Product design cycle

4 Category

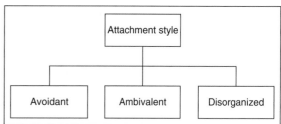

Figure 4: Parent-child attachment styles

5 Comparison/contrast

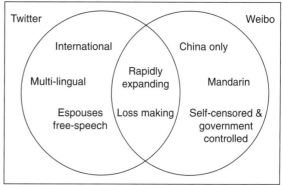

Figure 5: Comparison of Twitter and Weibo micro blogging services

6 Continuum

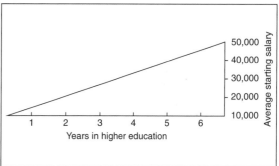

Figure 6: Relationship between education and starting salary

Exercise 7

Three extracts from texts that you have studied earlier are reproduced below. Make notes from the information in italics within each extract. Arrange each set of notes in the most appropriate diagram.

Extract 1

If two people are to progress in a relationship it will be because they gain from the way that they exchange benefits (i.e. rewards). [...] *Broadly speaking, resources exchanged include: goods, information, love, money, services and status Foa and Foa (1975).*

Source: Extracts from Vaughan & Hogg, Psychology © 2011 Pearson Australia pp 544–545, 537–538, 498.

Extract 2

Byrne and Clore have carried out extensive research dealing with the connection between sharing attitudes with another person and liking them (e.g. Byrne, 1971; Clore & Byrne, 1974). Attitudes that were markedly similar were an important ingredient in maintaining a relationship. *The results were so reliable and consistent that Clore (1976) formulated a 'law of attraction' – attraction towards a person bears a linear relationship to the actual proportion of similar attitudes shared with that person.* This law was thought to be applicable to more than just attitudes. Anything that other people do that agrees with your perception of things is rewarding, i.e. reinforcing. The more other people agree, the more they act as reinforcers for you and the more you like them.

Source: Extracts from Vaughan & Hogg, Psychology © 2011 Pearson Australia pp 544–545, 537–538, 498.

Extract 3

[...] increased Facebook use significantly predicts Facebook-related jealousy. We argue that this effect may be the result of *a feedback loop whereby using Facebook exposes people to often ambiguous information about their partner that they may not otherwise have access to and that this new information incites further Facebook use.*

Source: Extract from Muise, A., Christofides, E., & Desmarais, S. (2009). More Information than You Ever Wanted: Does Facebook Bring Out the Green-Eyed Monster of Jealousy? *CyberPsychology & Behavior, 12(4)*, 441–444.

Exercise 8

Read the text below, which describes a type of network commonly found in work places, and make notes in diagram form.

'The wheel, also sometimes known as the star, is the most centralized network. This network is the most efficient for simple tasks. Problems are solved more quickly with fewer mistakes and with fewer information flows. However, as the problems become more complex and demands on the link person increase, effectiveness suffers. The link person is at the centre of the network and acts as the focus of activities and information flows and the coordinator of group tasks. The central person is perceived as the leader of the group and experiences a high level of satisfaction. However, for members on the periphery, the wheel is the least satisfying network.'

Source: Extracts and table from *Management and Organisational Behaviour* by L J Mullins © 2010.

Making concise notes

Glossary

concise
Something that is concise says everything that is necessary without using any unnecessary words.

When you are making notes, it is important to note down the information with as few words as possible. Doing this will not only save you time, it will also help you avoid plagiarizing the source material.

For example:

Complete sentences	Concise notes
The 'Ringelmann effect' can be defined as the tendency to work less hard when part of a group than when working alone.	'Ringelmann effect' = tendency work less when in group
Transactional leadership is not the same as transformational leadership.	Transactional leadership ≠ transformational LS
An excessively directive leadership style can lead to loss of morale among subordinates.	Too directive LS → subordinates' morale ↓
Use of teamwork in organizations has increased. Therefore, managers need to be more flexible.	↑ teamwork ∴ more flexible managers
The ability to be both task-oriented and relationship-oriented is what makes a leader effective.	Task orientation + relationship ori. = effective LS

Tips To make concise notes:

- ✓ Avoid writing complete sentences.
- ✓ Focus on key content words, especially nouns, and the most important verbs, adjectives and adverbs.
- ✓ Do not include less important words such as articles ('a', 'an' and 'the').
- ✓ Use standard abbreviations if they are useful to you (such as e.g. = for example).
- ✓ Make your own abbreviations for words you commonly repeat.
- ✓ Use symbols to represent the relationships between ideas.

Research

Exercise 9

Cover the right hand column of the table on page 97 and practise rewriting the long versions in short note form using symbols and abbreviations. Come back to your short notes after a few days and turn them into sentences. Compare your sentences with the originals to check that you have kept the same meaning. Make sure that you have not left out any key information or misrepresented the original meaning. If you are in doubt ask a friend or your lecturer to compare what you have written with the original sentences.

For example:

You could make notes from the sentence: *An excessively directive leadership style can lead to loss of morale among subordinates.* in the following way:

lots of direction → loss of morale

If you later expand this into a sentence, you might produce: *A lot of direction leads to a loss of morale.*

If you compare this sentence with the original, you will see that the meaning of the original has not been adequately maintained. It is not just direction, but *too much* direction from leaders that is important; too much direction does not always lead to but *can* lead to loss of morale; and finally, loss of morale occurs not in general but specifically in subordinates.

You would be advised to go back to the original sentence and include a bit more of the key information in your notes.

Exercise 10

Read the extract below and make notes using the techniques described in this chapter. Use your notes to complete the missing information in the table in Exercise 6.

'There are, however, limitations to the situational approach. There are people who possess the appropriate knowledge and skills and appear to be the most suitable leaders in a given situation, but who do not emerge as effective leaders. Another limitation is that it does not explain fully the interpersonal behaviour or the different styles of leadership and their effects on members of the group. Finally, in the work organization, it is not usually practicable to allow the situation continually to determine who should act as a leader.

Despite the limitations of the situational approach, situational factors are important in considering the characteristics of leadership. More recent studies focus on the interactions between the variables involved in a leadership situation and patterns of leadership behaviour, and provide another general approach to the study of leadership – contingency theory [...]'

Source: Extracts and table from *Management and Organisational Behaviour* by L J Mullins © 2010.

Storing and retrieving notes

It is important to arrange your source materials and notes so that you can find the information again easily. If possible, store everything in one place. Label and file documents using a system that makes sense to you. For example, file copies of reading texts alphabetically by author's surname and file your notes under headings that come from your essay outline. Consider colour-coding your notes according to how relevant the information is to your essay. For example, if a note is to be used for background information, colour it blue, if it is to be referenced, colour it green, if it is to be quoted directly, colour it red.

If you prefer to work online, remember to periodically back up your files. Alternatively use web-based applications such as Evernote®, which allow you to save different types of files, including web pages, PDFs and word processed documents. This type of repository can generally be accessed with different devices, which can make retrieval of your documents more convenient.

Remember

✓ There is no one right or wrong way of making notes – the important thing is to practise and work out the best way for you.

✓ To save time note only the information that you need for your essay.

✓ Wherever possible, note the information in your own words keeping the author's original meaning.

✓ If you quote source material word-for-word, copy the extract accurately and use quotation marks " ".

✓ Always record bibliographic details, including page numbers.

✓ Make sure that you can distinguish between notes from the text and your own comments.

✓ Use different styles of note making for different types of information: outline, Cornell, table or diagram.

✓ Make your notes as concise as possible by omitting non-essential words and using abbreviations and symbols.

✓ Store your reading texts and notes in one place, using a filing system that makes sense to you.

✓ If your files are online, remember to back up regularly; consider using a web-based note management application.

9 | Writing an outline

Aims ✓ write outlines for different types of essay   ✓ structure introductions and conclusions

✓ devise an effective argument

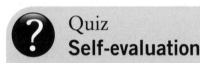

Quiz
Self-evaluation

Read the statements, then circle the word which is true for you.

1	I like to plan what I'm going to write by making an outline.	agree | disagree | not sure
2	I prefer to write my essay without an outline, developing my ideas as I go.	agree | disagree | not sure
3	I understand how to build an academic argument.	agree | disagree | not sure
4	I know what sort of points I need to put in the introduction.	agree | disagree | not sure
5	I know how to structure the main or middle section of different types of essay.	agree | disagree | not sure
6	I know what sort of points I need to put in the conclusion.	agree | disagree | not sure

Why write an outline?

Once you have finished information gathering, you need to decide how to approach the writing of your essay and in particular, whether you will write to a plan or outline. Some students write successful essays without writing an outline. For some, writing is a way of exploring ideas and discovering what they wish to say. As their argument takes shape, they may introduce structure to their essay through a process of redrafting.

Others find they achieve better results when they write an outline. Writing is a complex process. You have to consider many things at the same time: vocabulary, grammar, linking, paragraphing, use of source material and so on. As you are writing, you need to keep what you have already written in mind as well as think ahead to what you are going to write about next. Writing an outline is one way of making the process easier because you do not need to plan as you go. This means that you can focus on conveying your information clearly and effectively, using appropriate vocabulary and correct grammar.

Many students combine writing to an outline and free writing. They may start with a detailed outline and find that as they write, they discover new ways of presenting their ideas. They may then proceed with a revised outline. In any case, it is advisable to both plan ahead and remain open to changing your plan as you write.

What to include in your outline?

In its simplest form an outline is a list of the main points you intend to cover in your essay. Ideally, you will have prepared similar lists at earlier stages of the research process, for example, lists to organize your reading. When you create an outline at the writing up stage, it is helpful to include more detail: headings for main points, subheadings for subsidiary points, and notes from the source material you intend to include under each. How you arrange your headings depends on the type of essay you are writing. However, the structure of an essay is normally: general information in the introduction – specific information in the body – general points in the conclusion.

Exercise 1

A student has written an essay describing the main features of the Japanese graphic novel. In her essay, she has:

a described typical plot lines and character types

b explained why Japanese graphic novels are worth studying

c explained some of the common subtexts or hidden messages

d described common themes and imagery

e summarized the most significant features and indicated future trends

f given an overview of the historical context of the Japanese graphic novel

Which of these elements has she included in the introduction? Which in the conclusion? In which order do you think she covered the remaining subtopics in the body of her essay?

Essay introductions

It is worth taking the time to write a really effective introduction; it gives a favourable first impression of you as a writer and prepares the reader for the content of your essay. There are many possible ways of structuring an essay introduction; however, you should aim to achieve four main tasks, typically in the following order:

1   **Motivate your reader**

Reading an essay requires effort, so give your reader a reason to take an interest in your essay. You can do this by indicating that the topic of your essay is relevant, important and/or interesting. This is sometimes referred to as providing a 'rationale'.

> **For example:** An essay on altruism in humans might begin: *There has long been considerable interest in altruism, both among academics and the general public, centring on the issue of how altruistic human nature really is.*

2   **Contextualize your essay**

Your reader needs to know how this essay fits in with what they already know about the topic. To prepare your reader, give background information about the topic as well as a brief description of the research area. Remember that, although your only actual reader may be your lecturer, you should write your essay as if it were intended for other students on your course. You may therefore need to include some background information that is already known by your actual reader, i.e. your lecturer.

> **For example:** The essay on altruism might continue with: *Social psychological research into altruism started in the late 1950s and intensified in the 1960s following the notorious murder of a young woman called Kitty Gonovese in 1964. In the 25 years that followed, over 1000 scholarly articles on subject of altruism and helping behaviour were published. Today the issue is widely debated by not only social psychologists, but also by sociobiologists and evolutionary psychologists.*

3   **State your purpose**

You should clearly state the specific focus or purpose of your essay so that you can manage your reader's expectations. If your reader expects you to approach the topic in a different way, they may be confused and find it difficult to focus on the message that you are trying to convey. If you intend to investigate whether human beings are altruistic by nature, rather than, for example, how altruistic behaviour can be encouraged, you should state your intention clearly.

> **For example:** *The aim of this essay is to investigate the question of whether or not altruism is an innate human trait.*

Glossary

advocate
If you advocate a particular action or plan, you recommend it publicly.

4 Describe your plan

Briefly indicate how you plan to achieve your purpose so that your reader can easily follow your essay.

> **For example:** *The essay will begin by examining the evidence for and against the biological position. It will then consider the arguments put forward by scholars who advocate a social learning perspective.*

Exercise 2

Read the notes below for the introduction to the essay on leadership that you worked with in Chapter 8. Using the framework above, arrange the notes a–e in a suitable order.

a There are many ways of looking at leadership

b Aim: explain what 'good leadership' means in current era

c Over 400 definitions of leadership exist! (Crainer, 1995)

d 2 main theories discussed in this essay: Traits & Situational; recommendations given

e Success of organizations depends on effective leadership, especially in today's fast changing world

Organizing the body: Descriptive essays

If your essay question requires you to take a descriptive approach, organize the main body of your essay in whichever of the ways listed on the next page is most appropriate to the task. If you have to answer several different types of questions, use the most suitable approach for each section.

Describing main features

Glossary

principal
Principal means first in order of importance.

subtext
The subtext is the implied message or subject of something that is said or written.

If you simply have to describe something, organize your points under headings based on principal features.

For example:

If you are asked to describe the main features of the Japanese graphic novel, you might group points under headings such as:

Plot-lines

Character development

Use of imagery

Themes

Influences

Subtexts

Tips For descriptive essays, sequence your headings in a logical way:

✓ from general features to more specific features,
✓ from more important features to less important features,
✓ from more obvious features to less obvious features.

Tips

Describing events over time

If you have to present a narrative, you generally use a chronological structure.

For example:

If you are asked to trace the history of the graphic novel in Japan, you might group your points under headings such as:

Nineteenth century origins

Comic book art from 1900 to the 1930s

The post-war years

Generation X

Twenty-first century developments

Describing a process

If you have to describe a process, group your points into stages.

For example:

If you are asked to describe how graphic novels are created, you might organize your points under headings such as:

Selecting a visual style

Creating a storyboard

Scripting

Drawing

Comparing and contrasting information

Tasks which require you to compare and contrast information can be approached in two ways. Firstly, you can use a block approach, that is list all of the similarities between the two items and then list all of the differences (or vice versa).

For example:

If you want to compare Japanese and American graphic novels, you could arrange your points like this:

1 Similarities between Japanese and American graphic novels

    a idealization of the human figure

    b use of line and shading

    c themes of conflict and transformation

2 Differences between Japanese and American graphic novels

    a representation of emotion

    b use of colour

    c cultural references

Alternatively, you can compare the two items feature-by-feature.

> **For example:**
>
> 1 Character in Japanese and American graphic novels
>   a similarity: idealization of the human figure
>   b difference: representation of emotion
>
> 2 Visual style in Japanese and American graphic novels
>   a similarity: use of line and shading
>   b difference: use of colour
>
> 3 Thematic features of Japanese and American graphic novels
>   a similarity: conflict and transformation
>   b difference: cultural references

Exercise 3

Imagine you have been asked to compare and contrast the micro blogging service Twitter and its Chinese equivalent Weibo. Arrange the notes below using a block format and the headings: similarities and differences. Then reorganize the notes into a feature-by-feature format, creating your own headings. Decide which format will produce a better essay.

OVERVIEW: Micro blogging services

Twitter	Weibo
Started 2006	250m users in China; growing quickly (CNNIC, 2012)
Rapidly expanding; 140m active users (Twitter, 2012)	Started 2009
Promotes information exchange	Pioneered use of picture & video
Multi-lingual, worldwide	Effect: increases flow of information among users
Not profitable – posted $26m loss in 1st quarter 2012	Government monitoring & control; self-censorship encouraged (Buckley, 2011)
Users can post messages up to 140 characters + tweetpics & tweetvids since summer 2012	Posted $14m loss in 1st quarter 2011
Most popular use: socializing	Available in Mandarin only
Official policy of free speech, but since 2012 censorship laws in country of use apply (Twitter, 2012)	Users can post up to 140 characters + video & pictures
	Frequently used for socializing & for product information to aid purchasing decisions (CNNIC, 2012)

Organizing the body: Argument essays

Argument essays can be more challenging to structure because their purpose is not just to inform readers but to persuade them. Many students assume that writing an argument essay simply involves stating the arguments for and against a statement or proposal. In practice, argument essays in a university context require you to examine a range of perspectives, evaluate them, and synthesize ideas and information into a convincing message. A good academic argument should proceed step-by-step towards a conclusion that appears inevitable to the reader. This is quite a complex task. There are many different ways you can construct an argument. The approach illustrated in this chapter is one way, which you can adapt for a variety of argument essay questions.

Exercise 4

When organizing an argument essay, it is useful to think about the kinds of strategies that help people 'win' face-to-face arguments. In your opinion, how helpful are the strategies listed below?

1	Refuse to listen to your opponent's point of view.	helpful | unhelpful | not sure
2	Tell your opponent they are wrong without explaining why.	helpful | unhelpful | not sure
3	Admit that your opponent's point of view is reasonable in some ways.	helpful | unhelpful | not sure
4	Insist that your own views are perfect in every way.	helpful | unhelpful | not sure
5	Show how your point of view is connected to your opponent's point of view.	helpful | unhelpful | not sure
6	Give reasons and evidence to support your point of view.	helpful | unhelpful | not sure
7	Let your opponent speak, but try to have the last word.	helpful | unhelpful | not sure

Exercise 5

Look again at the notes for the essay critically examining two approaches to the study of leadership. These have been organized into an outline with two main headings: Traits approach and Situational theories, and four subheadings a–d for each.

1   What is the value of sequencing subheadings a–d in this way?

2   What is the connection between section 1d and section 2a?

3   Which approach do you think the writer favours – Traits or Situational?

---

1   Traits approach

   a   **Main feature**
Traits approach = leader's character most important; leaders born not made

   b   **Examples**
'self-confidence, initiative, intelligence and belief in one's actions' commonly seen as essential characteristics of effective leaders (Mullins, 2010: 377)

   c   **Support for traits approach**
many traits studies done 1904 to 1970; still influential

   d   **Problems with traits approach**
lists of traits produced by different studies tend to be overlapping, subjective & contradictory

difficult to say how particular personal qualities, e.g. charisma, contribute to firm's performance

some 'good' leaders successful in one situation but fail in others, e.g. Bob Horton of BP

2   Situational theories

   a   **Main features**
emphasis of situational theories: situation is important; no single style of leadership suitable for all situations

   b   **Examples**
Tannenbaum & Schmidt (1973) one of 1st to devise situational model

according to Tannenbaum & Schmidt (1973), some situations require 'boss-centred' leadership, others require 'subordinate-centred' leadership

   c   **Support for situational approach**
situational factors still considered significant

situational variables + leadership behaviour = contingency theory

   d   **Problems with situational approach**
right knowledge & abilities sometimes ≠ leadership

impact of differences in interpersonl style & leadership style not explained

not always feasible for situation → choice of leader

Tips To structure an academic argument:
  ✓ Move from 'weaker' to 'stronger' points of view.
  ✓ Explain how each new point of view is connected to your critical evaluation of previous points of view.
  ✓ Use this strategy to discuss theories, causes or effects, possible solutions to a problem and different interpretations of an artefact, such as a painting or poem.

Exercise 6

Think about a difficult situation that you are facing at the moment. Think of three possible solutions and list the advantages and disadvantages of each. Create an outline using what you have learned about building an academic argument.

Writing the conclusion

A strong conclusion is important. Because the conclusion is the last thing to be read, it is the part most likely to be remembered by the reader. Although the conclusion comes at the end of your essay, it can be seen as transitional: you look back at what you have written and look forward to what may happen in the future. In a conclusion, it is common to do some or all of the following:

1 Remind the reader of why the topic is useful, relevant or interesting.

   This reassures the reader that they have not wasted their time and effort in reading your paper.

2 Summarize the most important aspects of what you have written.

   This will help the reader remember the most important points and, if you are writing an argument essay, prepare your reader for your opinion (see point 3 below).

3 State your opinion on the topic (if appropriate).

   This is not always necessary in descriptive essays. However, for argument essays, it is the main part of your conclusion. It should follow on from your summary in a logical way and seem 'inevitable'.

4   Make recommendations for future action (if appropriate).

This is more common in argument essays within subjects such as management and engineering that have a practical focus. Here you indicate how what you have said in your essay could be applied in real life contexts.

5   Make recommendations for future research (if appropriate).

This feature is also more commonly found in argument essays. If you have pointed out the limitations of your preferred point of view, it is helpful to indicate in your conclusion how these limitations can be addressed. When you do this, you acknowledge that you have not said 'the last word' on the subject. This is how you hand the research question over to other researchers in the academic community.

Exercise 7

Read the notes below for the essay on leadership and, using the framework above, arrange them in a suitable order.

a   Both Traits & Situational approaches have limitations, but Situational more flexible, so more suitable for rapidly changing business environment.

b   Studies in future could investigate how well managers trained to adapt to different situations actually perform.

c   Main features of Traits & Situational approaches have been described, advantages & disadvantages of each have been examined.

d   These findings could be used in training programmes for managers & future leaders.

e   Important to understand what effective leadership means in increasingly challenging economic & political climate.

Tips   When applying essay frameworks:

✓   Remember that they are guidelines only. Frameworks can and should be used flexibly and adapted for particular essay questions.

✓   If your essay assignment requires you to answer several questions, use different patterns of organization for the different sections of your essay.

✓   Ideally, you should use frameworks and examples to help you develop your own approach to writing essay outlines.

Exercise 8

Look again at the essay question from Chapter 1 reprinted below. Write outline headings showing how you would structure the essay.

Figures published in 2012 by the Organization for Economic Co-operation and Development show considerable changes in the performance of secondary school pupils around the world in language, mathematics and science.

Compare and contrast the 2012 figures to those published in 2007 summarizing the most significant trends. To what extent can they be explained in terms of changes to national education policy? Discuss at least one additional factor that may have had a bearing on pupil performance.

Remember

✓ Avoid the need to plan as you write by preparing an outline before you write.

✓ Revise your outline as you discover new ideas and more effective ways of presenting your points.

✓ In your outline, include: headings for main sections, subheadings for subsidiary points, and notes from your source materials.

✓ Write a reader-friendly introduction: give a rationale, explain the context, state your purpose and summarize your plan.

✓ For descriptive writing, divide the body into manageable sections and sequence them in a logical way.

✓ For argument essays, sequence points of view from weakest to strongest; present each new point of view as a response to your critical analysis of the preceding point of view.

✓ Write the conclusion of an argument essay as if it were a 'bridge' to the future work of other researchers.

✓ Treat these guidelines flexibly; adapt them to suit your purpose.

10 Using sources

? Quiz
Self-evaluation

Read the statements, then circle T (true) or F (false).

1	An essay should contain mainly your own original ideas.	T | F
2	When you use information from other texts, you should usually quote it word-for-word.	T | F
3	To paraphrase a text, just change the key words.	T | F
4	When you summarize a text in your own words, you do not need to give the source.	T | F
5	If you use the ideas of a writer you agree with, you don't need to give the source.	T | F

What are source texts used for?

A source text is any text that you have used to help you write your essay. Research essays at undergraduate level are not generally required to contain completely original ideas. The expectation is that your essay will consist largely of ideas and information that you have gathered from other sources. The originality of your essay lies in the way that you combine, present and comment on that source material. The overall structure or argument of your essay should be your own; however, you normally use source texts to perform a wide variety of functions:

a **Define key terms**

How you define key terms often has an effect on the outcome of your argument. You should not always assume that scholars in your field

Glossary

concrete
You use concrete to indicate that something is definite and specific.

theoretical framework
A theoretical framework is a set of ideas used to analyse something or make judgements about it.

controversial
If you describe something or someone as controversial, you mean that they are the subject of intense public argument, disagreement, or disapproval.

expertise
Expertise is special skill or knowledge that is acquired by training, study, or practice.

define key terms in the same way. It is common, therefore, to present a selection of possible definitions taken from source texts and indicate which you intend to use in your essay.

b Give background information

Source material is often used, particularly in the introduction, to give background information about the topic and contextualize the essay. You use source material to show how what you have to say about the topic fits in with what other people have said about the topic.

c Provide evidence or examples to support a claim

This is one of the most common uses of source material. When you express an opinion or make a point, you need to support it with evidence. Some claims are better supported with statistical evidence. For example, the claim: 'Only a small proportion of reported crime results in a criminal conviction' should be supported with facts and figures. For other types of claim, examples or 'anecdotal evidence' may be sufficient. For example, the claim: *Some television news reports described those involved in the riots as 'animals',* could be supported with a few examples or quotes from news programmes.

d Give examples to illustrate a concept

Giving concrete examples to illustrate abstract concepts can make it easier for the reader to understand your point and see how it relates to everyday experience. Concrete examples can come from your own knowledge and experience or from your source materials; however, they must be clearly relevant to the point you are making.

e Present a theoretical framework

When you write at undergraduate or even master's degree level, you are unlikely to be asked to devise a theoretical framework of your own. If you have to apply or discuss a theory, it is likely to be one that you introduce via a source text.

f Present different points of view

When you are writing an argument essay, you need to show that you have considered the research question from more than one point of view. Source material is frequently used to represent different points of view.

g Support your own views with 'expert' opinion

It is also common to show that other people share your views about an issue. If you make a claim that is controversial, it is important to show that scholars with greater expertise would agree with you.

Research

Exercise 1

The extracts below come from a student essay about the problem of cybercrime and how it might be tackled. Match each extract 1–7 with one of the functions a–g listed on the previous page.

1   Rates of cybercrime have risen sharply. Data from the Internet Crime Complaint Centre show that there were just over 300,000 complaints registered in 2011, a six-fold increase over the 2001 figure (IC3, 2012).

2   Within the law-enforcement community, there is considerable disagreement about how precisely to define 'cybercrime'. Gordon and Ford (2006: 14) define it as any crime that is 'facilitated using a computer, network, or hardware device'.

3   The investigation of cybercrime has a long way to go. Indeed, according to Hunton (2011: 61), it is 'still in its infancy'.

4   The aim of the Cybercrime Execution and Analysis Model is to guide the decision making process involved in the investigation of highly complex cybercrime (Hunton, 2009).

5   When early precursors of the internet were developed by the US government in the 1970s, efforts were made to protect networks from cyber attack. During the early 1980s, an initial attempt was made to coordinate a global response to threats to the internet (Portnoy & Goodman, 2009: 5). Since then ...

6   In order to understand how a phishing attack works, consider the example of Kobe, who advertised a vehicle for sale on an online auction site ... (Gordon & Ford, 2006: 16–17).

7   Some experts advocate technological approaches to the problem of whitelisting (Zimsku, 2011). Others see the solution in terms of greater cooperation of national law enforcement agencies ...

Exercise 2

Now look at the paragraph below from the essay on cybercrime and answer questions 1–3.

1   How many source texts has the writer used, and what has he used each source for?

2   Which of the source texts has the writer paraphrased and which has he quoted word-for-word?

3   Why do you think the writer has paraphrased some source material and quoted other material?

'The incidence of cybercrime has increased significantly. Data from the Internet Crime Complaint Centre shows that online crime complaints in the United States increased substantially between 2007 and 2009 (IC3, 2010). The reported loss related to online fraud amounted to more than $550 million in 2009, twice the figure of the previous year (IC3, 2010). In the United Kingdom, a similar situation prevailed. Online banking fraud alone accounted for £59.7 million in losses, a 14 % rise on the 2008 figure (UKCA, 2010). These figures reinforce Smith *et al.'s* (2004: 35) contention that the internet has become a "playground for criminals".'

When to quote and when to paraphrase

Glossary

frame
When you frame information or a question, you arrange, express, or present it in a particular way for a particular purpose.

consistent
Someone who is consistent always behaves in the same way, has the same attitudes towards people or things, or achieves the same level of success in something.

When you are introducing source material into your essay, you need to decide whether to quote the material word-for-word or rewrite the information in your own words. For most types of essay, it is advisable to paraphrase or summarize material much more frequently than to quote it word-for-word. A ratio of one quote for every ten paraphrases or summaries is not uncommon. There are several reasons for this. Using your own words allows you to:

- demonstrate that you understand the source material,

- frame the information to make the point your want to make,

- maintain a consistent style.

Sometimes, however, it is appropriate to quote word-for-word. For some subject disciplines, such as law or literature, you are much more likely to use word-for-word quotes than in others.

Exercise 3

Read the paragraph below, which comes from the essay on cybercrime. In the spaces after each sentence:

- write NS if no source material is needed.

- indicate the function for any source material that is needed.

- indicate whether you would quote the source material word-for-word or paraphrase.

'The public perception of cybercrime is not the same as that of conventional crime, which people are much more likely to report to the police (1 _____). Consider, for instance, online banking fraud (2 _____). Although nowadays many banks encourage their customers to use online banking, the risk of online banking fraud has increased steadily (3 _____). However, when customers realise that they have become victims of online banking fraud, they generally report the crime directly to the bank rather than to the police (4 _____). If the amounts of money are small, the bank may not choose to involve the police (5 _____). Indeed, banks are reluctant to make incidents of online fraud known to outsiders because this could adversely affect confidence in the bank, and therefore profitability (6 _____).'

Tips

Tips   In general, you should consider quoting when:

✓   you want to comment on the language and not just the ideas of the source material.

✓   you are giving someone's definition of a key term.

✓   the language of the source material is special in some way (for example, creative, literary or well-known).

✓   you are referring to the law.

✓   the point being made in the source material is particularly controversial or could be easily misinterpreted.

How do I quote correctly?

Glossary

padding
Padding is unnecessary words or information used to make a piece of writing or a speech longer.

sic
You write sic in brackets after a word or expression when you want to indicate to the reader that although the word looks odd or wrong, you intended to write it like that or the original writer wrote it like that.

If you do decide to quote, you need to make sure you get the details right. If you have been given guidelines, use them. If not, follow the guidelines below:

1   Use only as much of the text as you need to make your point. If you include very long direct quotes where a shorter one would be sufficient, the person marking your essay could see this as 'padding'.

> For example, notice how the student has quoted more than is necessary from the 'Ringelmann effect' source text in Chapter 8:
>
> *'The Ringelmann effect can be understood in a number of ways. Mullins (2010: 353), for example, defines it simple as 'the tendency for individuals to expend less effort when working as a member of a group than as an individual. ~~A German psychologist, Ringelmann, compared the results of individual and group performance on a rope-pulling task~~.'*

2   Copy the text exactly. If you need to insert words to make the meaning of the quote clearer, put your own words in square brackets [ ]. If you need to omit some words use [...].

> For example, the student could have referred to the Mullins text in the following way:
>
> According to Mullins (2010: 353), 'the "Ringelmann effect" [...] is the tendency for individuals to expend less effort when working as a member of a group than as an individual.'

3   If the quote contains an error, copy the error adding [*sic*] after it.

> For example, in the quote below, the plural form of the word *crisis* is mistakenly used in place of the singular:
>
> *According to The Times, 'because so many regulators have oversight of the financial sector, there has been a crises [sic] of leadership.'*

4   Keep the original features of the text, such as capital letters and italics. If you want to draw attention to a word or words in the text yourself, you can put them in italics but write '(my emphasis)' at the end of the sentence before the final punctuation.

> For example, the Mullins quote could be presented as:
>
> 'Although the *total* amount of force did increase with the size of the work group, the effort expended by *each individual* member decreased' (my emphasis).

5   If the quote is short (three lines or fewer), put quotation marks around the material and write it in the body of your essay as normal. If the quote is embedded in a sentence of your own, make sure that the whole sentence is grammatically correct and coherent.

> For example, notice how the example given for point 2 would be a grammatically incorrect sentence fragment if presented as follows:
>
> *According to Mullins (2010: 353), '"the Ringelmann effect" which is the tendency for individuals to expend less effort when working as a member of a group than as an individual.'*

6   If the quote is longer than three lines, present it as a separate block of text without quotation marks, single spaced and indented from the body of your essay.

> **For example:**
>
> *Accounts of the Ringelmann experiment vary considerably. Mullins (2010: 354), for example gives the following account:*
>
> *A German psychologist, Ringelmann, compared the results of individual and group performance on a rope-pulling task. Workers were asked to pull as hard as they could on a rope, performing the task first individually and then with others in groups of varying size. A meter measured the strength of each pull.*

7   When you indicate in your reference where the quote came from, specify the page number. The examples given here use the 'Author-date' citation method. In this method, the page number of the quote is given after the year of publication in parentheses in the text of your essay.

> *According to Mullins (2010: 353), '"the Ringelmann effect" [...] is the tendency...'*

For more information on referencing, see Chapter 11.

Exercise 4

Read the extract below from a source text describing the impact of fraud or 'scams' on victims. Then read the extract from an essay in which the material has been quoted. What mistakes has the writer made?

Source material

'Scams cause psychological as well as financial harm to victims. Victims not only suffer a financial loss, but also a loss of self-esteem because they blame themselves for having been so 'stupid' to fall for the scam. Some of the victims we interviewed appeared to have been seriously damaged by their experience.'

Source: Extracts from The Psychology of Scams: Provoking and committing errors of judgement http://www.oft.gov.uk/shared_oft/reports/consumer_protection/oft1070.pdf.

Student essay

The impact of fraud on victims can be significant. According to the UK Office of Fair Trading (2009), 'Scams cause *psychological* as well as financial harm to victims. They not only suffer a financial loss, but also a loss of self-esteem because they blame themselves for having been so stupid to fall for the scam. Some of the victims interviewed appeared to have been seriously damaged by their experience'.

Paraphrasing and summarizing correctly

Paraphrasing and summarizing a text both involve rewriting the material in your own words. This does not mean simply changing key words. A paraphrase or summary should be a substantial reworking of the original text. The choice of words and grammar should be your own; however, your version should also retain the meaning and intent of the original source.

Generally speaking, a paraphrase retains more of the detailed information of the original text, whereas a summary is a more condensed version. In some disciplines, particularly in the sciences, it is much more common to summarize than to paraphrase.

Both paraphrasing and summarizing can be approached in a similar way:

1   Study the source material, focussing on what is most relevant to your essay.

2   Using your own words, make a few notes to help you retain the information you need.

3   Without looking at the source text, rewrite the material in your own words.

4 Compare your paraphrase or summary with the source text. Check that your version:

  a does not reproduce chunks of the original text,

  b is not a jumbled-up version of the original text,

  c does not distort the meaning or emphasis of the original text.

5 Check that your paraphrase or summary is clear and concise and connects smoothly and logically with the parts of your essay that come before and after.

6 Indicate the source of the information with a reference. Do this even if the source text contains ideas that are the same as your own.

If you find that your paraphrase or summary is not clear or contains too much of the original wording, this may be because you are still too focussed on the language of the source text rather than on the meaning.

Exercise 5

Following the steps above write a paraphrase of the source text in Exercise 4. Compare your version to the one in the answer key.

Tips To improve your paraphrasing, try the following:

  ✓ Read widely around your topic to become more familiar with the language used to describe it.
  ✓ Always write from notes, not from the source text.
  ✓ Allow time between note making from the source and writing your paraphrase or summary.
  ✓ Ask someone on your course or your lecturer to check that your paraphrase is clear and retains the meaning of the original source.
  ✓ Re-draft your paraphrase or summary after you have made your first attempt. Focus specifically on improving clarity.
  ✓ Imagine that you are writing for someone who is unable to understand the original text.
  ✓ Keep your paraphrase simple. Use shorter sentences and vocabulary that is familiar to you.

Keep in mind that although you should aim to use your own words wherever possible, there may be situations in which you have to copy some words because that is the set or usual way of representing the information. This is particularly true for technical and scientific writing.

Exercise 6

Read the student's paraphrase of the source text in Exercise 4. What problems do you notice?

Source text

Scams cause psychological as well as financial harm to victims. Victims not only suffer a financial loss, but also a loss of self-esteem because they blame themselves for having been so 'stupid' to fall for the scam. Some of the victims we interviewed appeared to have been seriously damaged by the experience. (Office of Fair Trading, 2009)

Paraphrase

'According to the UK Office of Fair Trading (2009: 8), harm is caused to victims by fraud, both psychological and financial. They may feel ashamed for having been so gullible, and as a consequence, lose not only money but also confidence in themselves. Some of the people we interviewed seemed to have been seriously damaged by their experience.'

Exercise 7

Imagine that you are writing an essay about the problem of mass-market fraud and how it might be addressed. Write a summary of up to 100 words of the source text below for inclusion in your essay.

Psychological reasons for responding to scams

The present research suggests that the psychological reasons for responding to scams involve a mixture of cognitive and motivational processes. Whilst different kinds of scam do exploit different vulnerabilities to some extent, there are similarities between scams in their content and the use of persuasive techniques. The greatest and most consistent emphasis was on:

■ appeals to trust and authority: people tend to obey authorities so scammers use, and victims fall for, cues that make the offer look like a legitimate one being made by a reliable official institution or established reputable business;

■ visceral triggers: scams exploit basic human desires and needs – such as greed, fear, avoidance of physical pain, or the desire to be liked – in order to provoke intuitive reactions and reduce the motivation of people to process the content of the scam message deeply. For example, scammers use triggers that make potential victims focus on the huge prizes or benefits on offer.

There are also a number of other error-inducing processes that emerged, including:

■ Scarcity cues. Scams are often personalized to create the impression that the offer is unique to the recipient. They also emphasize the urgency of a response to reduce the potential victim's motivation to process the scam content objectively;

■ Induction of behavioural commitment. Scammers ask their potential victims to make small steps of compliance to draw them in, and thereby cause victims to feel committed to continue sending money;

- The disproportionate relation between the size of the alleged reward and the cost of trying to obtain it. Scam victims are led to focus on the alleged big prize or reward in comparison to the relatively small amount of money they have to send in order to obtain their windfall; a phenomenon called 'phantom fixation'. The high value reward (often life-changing, medically, financially, emotionally or physically) that scam victims thought they could get by responding, makes the money to be paid look rather small by comparison.

Source: Extracts from The Psychology of Scams: Provoking and committing errors of judgement http://www.oft.gov.uk/shared_oft/reports/consumer_protection/oft1070.pdf.

Remember

✓ Use material from source texts in your essay introduction to provide a context and define key terms.

✓ Use material from source texts to illustrate abstract concepts and support claims.

✓ Use source texts to support your own point of view and to introduce alternative points of view.

✓ Paraphrase or summarize source material unless you have a good reason to quote word-for-word.

✓ Quote word-for-word if there is something special about the language of the source text or if the point it makes is controversial.

✓ When you quote word-for-word, accurately copy only as much of the source text that you need in order to make your point.

✓ Put short quotes in quotation marks; make quotes longer than three lines stand out from the rest of your essay by using single spacing and indenting.

✓ When paraphrasing or summarizing, use your own words, but keep standard technical or scientific expressions as they are in the original source text.

✓ Check that the language that you use in your summary or paraphrase is clear, accurate and substantially different from the language of the original text.

✓ Check that your quote, paraphrase or summary fits with the rest of your essay in terms of grammar, style and purpose.

✓ Give references for all quotes, paraphrases and summaries.

11 | Referencing

Aims ✓ recognize different referencing systems

✓ reference using an author-date system

✓ reference with footnotes

✓ know when a reference is and is not needed

Aims

? Quiz
Self-evaluation

Read the statements, then circle the word which is true for you.

1	I can recognize different referencing systems.	agree | disagree | not sure
2	I know which referencing system I need to use.	agree | disagree | not sure
3	I know the difference between a bibliography and a list of sources.	agree | disagree | not sure
4	I know when I need to reference.	agree | disagree | not sure

What referencing system should I use?

Whenever you use source material in your essay, whether paraphrased, summarized or quoted word-for-word, you need to indicate where the source material came from. In other words, you need to give a reference. Not giving references is considered plagiarism, that is, dishonestly presenting the work of other people as if it were your own. If you are seen to deliberately plagiarize, you will be penalized.

For more information on plagiarism and how to avoid it, see Chapter 12.

There are many different referencing systems. Each discipline prefers certain systems to others. Most departments specify which system they want to use and/or provide their own guidelines. If you need to write essays for different disciplines, you may need to learn several different referencing systems.

Although there is a great deal of variation in referencing systems, they all work in similar ways. Each specifies how you should:

a   indicate the presence of source material in the text of your essay.

b   list the sources that you have used at the end of your essay.

This chapter illustrates the main features of two commonly used systems, author-date and footnote-bibliography, as set out in the *Chicago Manual of Style*.

Tips
- ✓ Ask your university department for guidance on which referencing system to use.
- ✓ If you do not have guidelines, follow the system most commonly used in your source materials.
- ✓ Apply your chosen referencing guidelines consistently and accurately.

Author-date system in-text citations

The author-date system is widely used in the social sciences and in some scientific disciplines. Variations of the system include the American Psychological Association (APA) and the Harvard style. As the name implies, author-date systems indicate the presence of source material in the text by giving the author's surname and the date of publication. Notice in the example below how this is done in the *Chicago Manual of Style* version.

'There is some evidence to support the commonly held view that online social networking has a negative impact on face-to-face social relationships and psychological health. Chou and Edge (2012) found that people who make extensive, as opposed to occasional, use of Facebook were significantly more likely to regard others as happier than themselves. Facebook use has also been associated with heightened feelings of jealousy within romantic relationships (Muise, Christofides and Desmarais, 2009).

The findings of other researchers, however, have challenged the view that internet use is harmful. According to the social psychologists Hogg and Vaughan (2011, 603), internet users 'do not become lonely or depressed, or withdraw from interacting socially with others in real-life settings'. Moreover, the Australian Psychological Society (2010) report that online social networking can actually increase social contact and face-to-face social activity, resulting in improved well-being for many users.'

Glossary

et al.
et al. is used after a name or a list of names to indicate that other people are also involved. It is used especially when referring to books or articles which were written by more than two people.

Points that you should think about when writing in-text citations are listed below:

- If the source text was written by two authors, you should write both surnames. For example: *Chou and Edge* ... For three authors, write all three surnames. Note that in English speaking countries, we normally write the given name followed by the surname. On the title page of the article referred to, for example, the authors' names are written as *Hui-Tzu Grace Chou* and *Nicholas Edge*, but in the in-text citation only *Chou and Edge* are used.

- If the source text was written by four or more authors, write the surname of the first author followed by 'et al.' For example: (*Smith et al. 2012*).

- If the authors' names are part of the sentence, give the year of publication in round brackets immediately after the names. For example: *Chou and Edge (2012) found* ...

- If the authors' names are not part of the sentence, place them along with the date of publication in round brackets at the end of the sentence. Put the final punctuation after the bracket. For example: ... *within romantic relationships (Muise, Christofides and Desmarais, 2009)*.

- When you quote word-for-word, give the page number(s) after the year of publication. For example: *Hogg and Vaughan (2011, 603)*.

- If you need to refer to a source, for example Bryan and Test (1967), that is mentioned in another source, for example in Hogg and Vaughan (2011), you would write the in-text citation as follows: *(Bryan and Test 1967 cited in Hogg and Vaughan 2011)*. Note, however, that wherever possible, you should try to find the original source and reference it directly.

Exercise 1

Look at the textbook extracts in Chapter 5 for examples of author-date referencing in the APA style. What differences do you notice (if any) between APA and *Chicago Manual of Style* in-text citations?

Author-date style reference list

At the end of your essay you normally list all of the references you have used alphabetically by the author's surname. Examples of three different types of source texts are given below along with a description of their component parts. Study these carefully. Notice the layout, punctuation and use of upper case letters.

Journal article

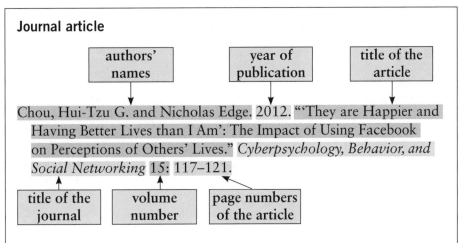

Chou, Hui-Tzu G. and Nicholas Edge. 2012. "'They are Happier and Having Better Lives than I Am': The Impact of Using Facebook on Perceptions of Others' Lives." *Cyberpsychology, Behavior, and Social Networking* 15: 117–121.

Notice that:

- The first author's surname is given first, followed by the given name. The second author's name is written as normal.

- The title of the article is put in quotation marks.

- The title of the journal is in italics.

Book

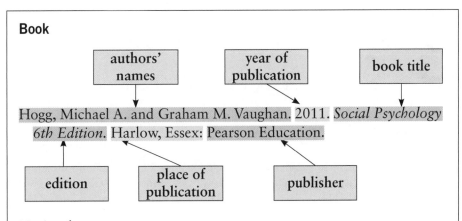

Hogg, Michael A. and Graham M. Vaughan. 2011. *Social Psychology 6th Edition.* Harlow, Essex: Pearson Education.

Notice that:

- The title of the book is in italics.

- The edition of the book is mentioned. This is not necessary if you are using the first edition of the book.

- You can find the edition number on the front cover of a book; for the year of publication check the title page for the year that corresponds with the edition you are using. Ignore imprint numbers.

Glossary

commission
if you commission something or commission someone to do something, you formally arrange for someone to do a piece of work for you.

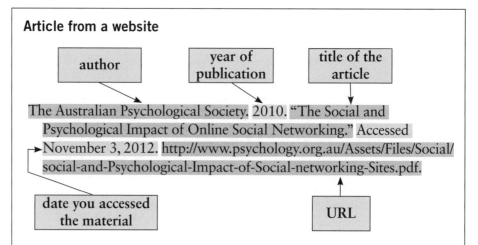

Article from a website

author → year of publication → title of the article

The Australian Psychological Society. 2010. "The Social and Psychological Impact of Online Social Networking." Accessed November 3, 2012. http://www.psychology.org.au/Assets/Files/Social/social-and-Psychological-Impact-of-Social-networking-Sites.pdf.

date you accessed the material ↑   URL ↑

Notice that:

- The name of the organization that commissioned the report is given in place of the author because, in this case, the person who wrote the report is not named.

- The date the material was accessed is given along with the date of publication.

Exercise 2

Study the reference below. What type of source is it? Label its component parts.

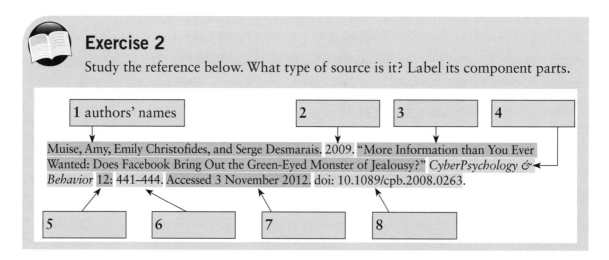

1 authors' names   2   3   4

Muise, Amy, Emily Christofides, and Serge Desmarais. 2009. "More Information than You Ever Wanted: Does Facebook Bring Out the Green-Eyed Monster of Jealousy?" *CyberPsychology & Behavior* 12: 441–444. Accessed 3 November 2012. doi: 10.1089/cpb.2008.0263.

5   6   7   8

There are many different types of sources available nowadays. Referencing guidelines are frequently updated as new types of sources, particularly online sources, become more widely used.

Exercise 3

Log onto the *Chicago Manual of Style* website at http://www.chicagomanualofstyle.org/home.html. Using the 'quick search' facility, find examples showing how to list the four sources below.

1   a chapter in an edited book

2   an e-book

3   a book review (online)

4   an article in a newspaper

Exercise 4

Correct the errors in the reference list below.

G. L. Clore and D. Byrne. "A Reinforcement-affect Model of Attraction." In *Foundations of Interpersonal Attraction*, 1974, edited by T. L. Huston, 143-165. Academic Press: New York.

Rusbult C. E., J. M. Martz and C. R. Agnew 1998 The Investment Model Scale: Measuring Commitment Level, Satisfaction Level, Quality of Alternatives, and Investment Size *Personal Relationships* 5 357-391

Smahel, David, Bradford B. Brown, and Lucas Blinka. 2012. "Association between online friendship and Internet addiction among adolescents and emerging adults." Developmental Psychology 48: pages 381-388. doi 10.1037/a0027025. Accessed March 3, 2013.

Referencing with footnotes

Footnotes are commonly used in law and in many disciplines in the humanities. In this style of referencing, in-text citations are indicated with small numbers placed immediately after the source material or, if the author of the source is mentioned in the text of the essay, immediately after the author's name. Bibliographic details are given at the bottom of the page (footnotes) or at the end of the essay (in which case they are referred to as endnotes). Here's how the sample text given earlier would appear with footnotes:

> 'There is some evidence to support the commonly held view that online social networking has a negative impact on face-to-face social relationships and psychological health. Chou and Edge[1] found that people who make extensive, as opposed to occasional, use of Facebook were significantly more likely to regard others as happier than themselves. Facebook use has also been associated with heightened feelings of jealousy within romantic relationships[2].
>
> The findings of other researchers, however, have challenged the view that internet use is harmful. According to the social psychologists Hogg and Vaughan[3], internet users 'do not become lonely or depressed, or withdrawn from interacting socially with others in real-life settings'. Moreover, the Australian Psychological Society[4] report that online social networking can actually increase social contact and face-to-face social activity, resulting in improved well-being for many users.'
>
> ---
>
> [1] Hui-Tzu G. Chou and Nicholas Edge, "'They are Happier and having Better Lives than I Am': The Impact of Using Facebook on Perceptions of Others' Lives," *Cyberpsychology, Behavior, and Social Networking* 15 (2012): 121.
>
> [2] Amy Muise, Emily Christofides, and Serge Desmarais, "More Information than You Ever Wanted: Does Facebook Bring Out the Green-Eyed Monster of Jealousy?" *CyberPsychology & Behavior* 12 (2009): 441, accessed November 3, 2012, doi.10.1089/cpb.2008.0263.
>
> [3] Michael A. Hogg and Graham M. Vaughan, *Social Psychology 6th Edition* (Harlow, Essex: Pearson Education, 2011), 603.
>
> [4] "The Social and Psychological Impact of Online Social Networking," 2012, The Australian Psychological Association, accessed November 3, 2012, http://www.psychology.org.au/Assets/Files/Social-and-Psychological-Impact -of-Social-Networking-Sites.pdf.

Subsequent references to these sources are given in shortened form. For example, if page 42 of the first item were referred to later in the essay, the footnote would be written as:

Chou and Edge, "Impact of Using Facebook," 42.

If page 41 of the same text is mentioned again immediately afterwards, the abbreviation 'ibid.' can be used in place of the authors' names and the title of the publication. **For example:** Ibid. 41.

If page 43 of the same work is referred to elsewhere in the essay (but not immediately after being mentioned previously), the abbreviation 'op. cit.' can be used instead of the title of the publication. **For example:** Chou and Edge, op. cit. 43.

Glossary

op. cit.
op. cit. is used after an author's name to refer to a work of theirs which has already been mentioned.

Writing the bibliography

When referencing with footnotes, the list of references at the end of the essay is commonly referred to as a bibliography. This is how the works cited above would appear in the bibliography.

Chou, Hui-Tzu G. and Nicholas Edge. "'They are Happier and Having Better Lives than I Am': The Impact of Using Facebook on Perceptions of Others' Lives." *Cyberpsychology, Behavior, and Social Networking* 15 (2012): 117–121.

Hogg, Michael A. and Graham M. Vaughan. *Social Psychology 6th Edition*. Harlow, Essex: Pearson Education, 2011.

Muise, Amy, Emily Christofides, and Serge Desmarais. "More Information than You Ever Wanted: Does Facebook Bring Out the Green-Eyed Monster of Jealousy?" *CyberPsychology & Behavior* 12 (2009): 441–444. Accessed November 3, 2012. doi.10.1089/cpb.2008.0263.

The Australian Psychological Society. "The Social and Psychological Impact of Online Social Networking." 2010. Accessed November 3, 2012. http://www.psychology.org.au/Assets/Files/Social-and-Psychological-Impact-of-Social-Networking-Sites.pdf.

Exercise 5

What are the main differences between the footnote entries and bibliography entries for the four items listed on the previous page?

The word 'bibliography' is sometimes used to refer to a list of sources which also includes texts that have been looked at but not specifically cited in the text. A list of references, in contrast, always contains only items cited in the text. Sometimes books, journal articles and other types of documents are listed in separate sections.

Tips   Ask your department for guidance on whether you need to:
✓ write a bibliography or a list of references,
✓ list items alphabetically or according to type.

Do I always need to reference?

When you quote, summarize or paraphrase from a source text, you must give a reference. However, this does not mean that you have to reference everything in your essay that you have read in a source text. Some of what you read may be 'common knowledge', that is knowledge that is not considered to 'belong' to a particular person or persons. When you make statements expressing common knowledge using your own words, you do not have to give a reference, even if you happen to have read similar statements in other texts. Sometimes it is easy to recognize common knowledge; however, sometimes it can be difficult to distinguish between common knowledge and information that is the intellectual property of the author of the text.

Tips

✓ If you notice that many authors make the same point without referring to a source, you are probably dealing with common knowledge.

✓ If you are not sure whether or not an idea of piece of information is common knowledge, treat it as source material and give the reference.

Exercise 6

The sentences below come from a student essay about cybercrime. Which do you think express common knowledge? Which do you think contain information or ideas that belong to a specific author?

1 People who communicate personal and financial information via the internet can become the targets of cybercriminals.

2 Cybercrime has a damaging effect on the individuals and organizations that have been targeted.

3 New York has a larger number of e-commerce fraud victims than any other city in the United States.

4 Cybercriminals are becoming increasingly sophisticated.

5 Fifteen per cent of recorded cybercrime involves identity theft.

Remember

✓ Ask your department or course leader for guidance on referencing.

✓ Be prepared to learn different referencing systems if you are writing across academic disciplines.

✓ Once you know which system to use in your essay, apply it consistently.

✓ Pay attention to detail; be consistent in your use of punctuation.

✓ If you are using an author-date system, use the author's surname and date in in-text citations; for direct quotes, give the page number after the date.

✓ In the list of references, list source texts alphabetically by the author's surname.

✓ If you are using a footnote-bibliography system, learn to use abbreviations such as 'ibid.' and 'op. cit.' for repeated references to the same source.

✓ Learn to distinguish between common knowledge, which you do not necessarily need to reference if you express it in your own words, and intellectual property, which you must always reference.

12 | Finding your voice

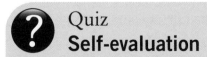

? Quiz
Self-evaluation

Tick the statements that are true for you.

1	I worry about plagiarism.	
2	I don't like using my own words in my essay because my language skills are not very good.	
3	I feel nervous about expressing my opinion in my essay because I am not an expert.	
4	I worry that if I have too many references, the essay will not be seen as my own work.	
5	I'm not sure whether to use 'I' in my essay.	
6	I'm not sure how I should express my opinion in my essay.	

Using source material correctly

Glossary

deliberate
If you do something that is deliberate, you planned or decided to do it beforehand, and so it happens on purpose rather than by chance.

One of the biggest challenges facing you as a researcher is learning to combine your own ideas with the ideas you have gathered from your sources to create a unified message. It is important that you do not lose your 'voice' – that is, your ideas and your way of expressing yourself. It is also important that you properly represent the material in your essay that comes from other scholars.

Proper use of sources, and in particular, the need to avoid plagiarism, is a concern for most people learning to do research. But what exactly is plagiarism? We often define plagiarism as deliberately presenting other people's words and ideas as if they were your own. However, plagiarism can take many forms and is not always deliberate.

Exercise 1

Which of the practices 1–5 could be considered plagiarism?

1   Paraphrasing source texts by substituting key words and changing the order of the sentences.

2   Listing all of the references used at the end of the essay but not giving in-text citations.

3   Giving the reference for material that has been quoted word-for-word but not using quotations marks.

4   Drawing most of your source material from one or two texts.

5   Using material that has been written by another student.

Some people plagiarize because they believe it is a common practice and that they are unlikely to be caught. However, plagiarism is often easy to detect. Moreover, the penalties for plagiarizing can be severe; you can even be asked to leave your university.

Exercise 2

Read the extract below from an essay written by a student from Japan about mobile phone communication in her country. Underline the section that you think has been plagiarized.

'In Japan the personal communication media developed in unique way and resulted that people adopted online communication quickly. First cellular phone service began in Japan in 1979, which was a quite early phenomenon compared to rest of world. The develop of telecommunication encouraged people to be interested in internet. The main use of mobile phone is exchange e-mail between friends and relatives (Ishii, 2002). Although a limited form of contact, mobile e-mail has fulfilled a function akin to co-presence for people who lack the means to share the same private physical space (Ito, 2005: 16). Therefore, young people in Japan dependant on mobile phone and online communication.'

One aspect of the internet addiction among Japanese youths is the phenomenon 'internet café refugees'. People have no fixed accommodation sometimes taking refuge in internet cafés which open 24/7 and provide the food, drink and access to the toilet facilities. Due to Japanese tendency of associating internet with privacy, these cafés are not designed as an open space but a collection of booths and privacy rooms. This arranging of space increases problem of internet addiction and the social isolation. Other manifestation of internet addiction is referred as *hikikomori*. *Hikikomori* doesn't have English translation but maybe can describe as a person who spend all of their time at home online, doesn't has interest in school or work, and suffering from more than one mental disorder (Ministry of Health, Labour and Welfare Japan, 2003 in Teo and Gaw, 2010) …

Why do people plagiarize?

Glossary

misconception
A misconception is an idea that is not correct.

Most people know that it is wrong to plagiarize. However, sometimes people plagiarize because they have some other difficulty.

Sometimes the difficulty comes from unrealistic expectations. Some students believe that the language they use in their essays must be as sophisticated and error-free as the language they read in academic books and articles. They plagiarize because they fear that if they use their own language, the end result will not be acceptable.

Another common misconception is that an essay must be full of brilliant original ideas. Students who believe this sometimes present other scholars' ideas as if they were their own because they worry they have nothing special or new to say about the subject.

Lack of skills and problems with time management can also result in plagiarism. As you may have discovered in the preceding chapters of this book, you need a wide range of skills to handle sources correctly. It takes time and a lot of practice to master them. Writing a research essay is also a lengthy process. If you delay, you have to write under pressure, which increases the temptation to plagiarize.

Avoiding plagiarism

Glossary

overwhelming
If something is overwhelming it affects you very strongly, and you do not know how to deal with it.

perfectionist
Someone who is a perfectionist refuses to do or accept anything that is not as good as it could possibly be.

Because the reasons that people plagiarize are often very different, the question *How do you avoid plagiarism?* has many answers.

Certainly, having realistic expectations is a good start. Remember that students are not expected to write as if they were professional writers or experienced academics. While a reasonable level of accuracy in writing is an advantage, the content and quality of your thinking are much more important. In terms of language, most markers are looking for clarity rather than sophistication. As long as you avoid obviously informal language, your normal 'voice' should be good enough.

If you usually feel tempted to plagiarize because you write in a hurry, make sure you allow yourself enough time to do the job adequately. If you find the size of the task overwhelming, break it down into manageable stages and set yourself realistic deadlines for each stage. Prioritize important tasks and try not to be a perfectionist.

If lack of skills is your problem, keep practising. Read academic texts not just for their content but also for examples of how other writers in your subject discipline handle sources. If your course allows you to use anti-plagiarism software to check your work before submitting it, use it as a learning aid. Most programmes work by highlighting the text in your essay that is similar to text stored in their database. This allows you to see where you need to make changes such as adding references or quotation marks, or rewriting inadequately paraphrased material.

Tips Ways to reduce the risk factors of plagiarism.

✓ Have realistic expectations about the level of originality and language required.
✓ Manage your time well; do not write in a hurry.
✓ Study how other writers handle source material.
✓ Learn to use anti-plagiarism software.

Finally, if you feel the need to plagiarize because you worry that what you have to say is not good enough, have the confidence to take control of your essay. Respect the work of other scholars but do not be too timid or lose confidence in yourself. Remember that for argument essays in particular, your opinions and critical commentary are highly valued. What you say about your topic and source materials does not necessarily need to be 'correct' – or completely original. What is important is that you show that you have made a thoughtful investigation of the topic and that you can support your ideas with evidence.

Tips Here are some practical steps that you can take to stay in control of your essay.

✓ Make sure the topic sentence of each paragraph is in your own words and expresses your own idea.
✓ Make sure that when you include source material, you have a clear idea of what you are using it for.
✓ In general, avoid using very long direct quotes.
✓ Comment on the quotes that you do use.
✓ If you compare and contrast two points of view, give your own point of view too.
✓ For argument essays, make up your mind on the issue and argue the case. Although extreme opinions are harder to defend and should therefore generally be avoided, you should also avoid 'sitting on the fence' (= not supporting a particular side in a discussion or argument).

Can I use 'I' in my essay?

One of the aspects of academic writing that can make it difficult for you to find your 'voice' is the need to maintain an objective tone. For many disciplines, this includes avoiding the use of personal pronouns, in

Research

particular 'I'. It is not surprising that students often ask: *How can I express my opinion without using expressions like 'I think' or 'in my opinion'?*

Generally speaking, there is no need for these expressions if you consider the essay as a whole to be an expression of your opinion. It may be helpful to think of it this way: the reader will assume that every statement you write is your opinion unless it is obviously common knowledge or unless you give a reference.

Rather than writing: *I think that students learn better when they feel empowered*, use an 'it' or 'there' phrase to express your opinion: for example, *It is clear that students learn better when they feel empowered* or *There is good reason to believe that students learn better when they feel empowered*. Then back up your claim with evidence.

However, note that in some subjects such as nursing, students are often asked to reflect on personal and professional experience in their essays. In these cases, it is not only allowable but necessary to use 'I'.

Tips Ask your department for guidance on using 'I' in your essay. If you need to avoid expressions like 'I think', use:

✓ 'it is + adjective', e.g. 'it is likely that …'
✓ 'there is + noun', e.g. 'there is strong evidence that …'

Exercise 3

Rewrite sentences 1–4 using the structure *it* + adjective or *there* + noun. Use the words in brackets in your answers.

1 I had to investigate further.

   It _____ . [necessary]

2 I would prefer to have a shorter working week and fewer redundancies even if that means lower take-home pay.

   It _____ . [preferable]

3 I predict that within the next five years, schoolchildren will be using mobile devices to learn basic skills in the classroom.

   It _____ . [likely]

4 I don't have enough evidence to establish a clear link between frequent online gaming and hyperactivity.

   There is _____ . [insufficient evidence]

Exercise 4

Compare the two paragraphs below from the essay on cybercrime. Answer questions 1–3.

1 What is the purpose of each citation?

2 In which paragraph does the writer appear to be more in control?

3 How does the writer express his opinion in the second paragraph without using 'I'?

Paragraph 1

'Wall (2003) divided cybercrime into three categories. Firstly, there is traditional cybercrime, which is common traditional crimes that are committed using the internet, such as: fraud, stalking and so on. Secondly, there is hybrid cybercrime, defined as online criminal acts which enable perpetrators to commit traditional crimes. Hacking and ID theft are examples of this. Thirdly, there is true cybercrime, where criminals make new opportunities for new types of crime, for example, phishing, intellectual property piracy and so on.'

Paragraph 2

'The incidence of cybercrime has increased significantly. Online crime complaints in the United States increased substantially between 2007 and 2009 (IC3, 2010). In the United States, the reported loss related to online fraud amounted to more that $550 million in 2009, twice the figure of the previous year (IC3, 2010). In the United Kingdom, a similar situation prevailed. Online banking fraud alone accounted for £59.7 million in losses, a 14% rise on the 2008 figure (UKCA, 2010). These figures reinforce Smith *et al*.'s (2004: 35) contention that the internet has become a "playground for criminals"'.

Forms of citation

Notice how in the examples above, the citations have been presented in different ways: sometimes the source author's name appears as the subject of the sentence, at other times, it appears in parentheses at the end of the sentence. These differences are significant because they allow you to 'frame' the source material and, in doing so, influence the way the reader perceives it.

The first and last citations, 'Wall (2003) divided ...' and 'Smith *et al*.'s (2004: 35) contention ...' are commonly referred to as 'author-prominent' citations. If you use this form of citation, you emphasize that what is being presented is specifically the author's action or opinion. Author-prominent citations usually involve using a reporting verb, which allows you to indicate the nature of the source material that you are presenting.

For example, you can use a range of reporting verbs to refer to aspects of the research process: 'estimate', 'calculate', and 'find'. *Carter et al. (2012) found that the incidence of credit card fraud had been underestimated by at least 50 per cent.*

Other reporting verbs, such as 'think', 'believe', and 'consider', refer to thinking processes. *Smith et. al. (2004: 35) believe that the internet has become a "playground for criminals".*

Other verbs indicate the form of communication, for example: 'write', 'argue', and 'state'. *Granger (2011) states that identity theft is on the rise.*

The reporting verbs above are all neutral in the sense that they indicate the nature of the material but do not convey your opinion of it. Other reporting verbs allow you to convey something of your opinion of the source material. For example, if you write: *Smith et al. (2004: 35) claim that the internet has become a "playground for criminals"*, you convey scepticism. If, on the other hand you want to indicate that that the source material is valid in your opinion, you can use other verbs such as: 'show', 'establish', and 'demonstrate'.

Exercise 5

Indicate how each of the reporting verbs 1–5 changes the writer's opinion in the following sentence: 'Smith *et al.* (2004: 35) _____ that the internet has become a "playground for criminals"'.

1 suggest	2 assume	3 imply	4 demonstrate	5 allege

The other main form of citation is commonly referred to as 'information prominent'. In this form of citation, the source material is presented first, and the reference follows. There are three examples of information prominent citations in the second paragraph in Exercise 4: … 'increased substantially between 2007 and 2009 (IC3, 2010)' '… twice the figure of the previous year (IC3, 2010)' and '… a 14% rise on the 2008 figure (UKCA, 2010)'. As the name suggests, this form of citation emphasizes the information in the source material rather than the author. It is often used to present information as 'fact' rather than as opinion. In some disciplines, in the sciences for example, virtually all citations take this form.

Exercise 6

Skim read a section of a book or article in your subject discipline focussing on the form of citation used. Answer questions 1–2.

1   What is the proportion of author-prominent to information-prominent citations?
2   If author prominent citations are present, what reporting verbs are used?

Exercise 7

Imagine you are writing a paragraph about the reasons why people become attracted to one another and form social relationships. Re-read the textbook extracts in Chapter 5 and choose two of them to use as your source materials.

Decide which text offers the more convincing explanation. Then:

1   Write a topic sentence introducing the content of your paragraph.
2   Paraphrase or quote from the two source texts using the most appropriate form of citation for each – author prominent or information prominent.
3   Give your own commentary of each source.
4   Write a concluding sentence summarizing your opinion.

Remember

✓   Learn to recognize and avoid plagiarism in all its forms.

✓   Have a realistic understanding of what 'originality' and 'good writing' mean in your study context.

✓   Manage your time well so that you do not need to write under too much pressure.

✓   Practise the skills needed to use sources well; notice how others in your field do it.

✓   If you have access to anti-plagiarism software through your course, use it to help you identify where you are going wrong.

✓   Have the confidence to express your opinion.

✓   Take control of your paper by writing your own topic sentences and being clear about what you want to say with your source materials.

✓   Remember that your opinions and critical commentary on your source material are highly valued.

✓   Use different citation styles to frame the source material in the way that best conveys your message.

13 | Writing up

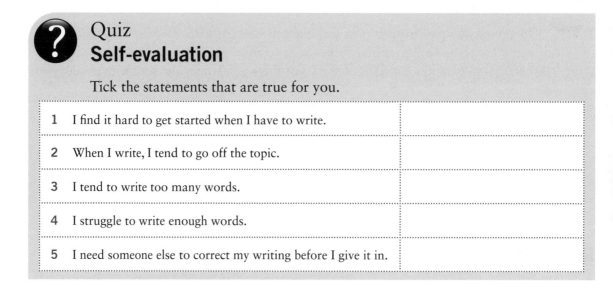

? Quiz
Self-evaluation

Tick the statements that are true for you.

1	I find it hard to get started when I have to write.	
2	When I write, I tend to go off the topic.	
3	I tend to write too many words.	
4	I struggle to write enough words.	
5	I need someone else to correct my writing before I give it in.	

Getting started

If getting started is particularly difficult, this may be for one of several reasons. Sometimes it is difficult to know when to stop reading and gathering information and when to start writing. Some writers feel they need to read everything available about the topic before they write; others get stuck because they feel they must write a 'perfect' essay right from the start.

One way around this is to write a first draft with the aim of simply getting your ideas down on paper. Whether you work from an outline or not, write as freely as you can without pausing to make corrections. You can then redraft your essay section by section.

Staying on topic

If your difficulty is not in starting but in staying within the boundaries of your topic, it is important that you learn to stay focussed. Writing off topic, even if you write well and have something interesting to say, can result in a significantly lower mark.

Tips
- ✓ Give yourself enough thinking and planning time before you write.
- ✓ Work to an outline.
- ✓ Display your essay question where you can see it easily.
- ✓ Underline the key words in your title to keep you focussed.
- ✓ Before you write each section, re-read your essay question, pause and think.

Using assessment criteria to redraft

Remember that, in most cases, the person who marks your essay will use assessment criteria to evaluate what you have done. After you have written a first draft, it is a good idea to remind yourself of the criteria that will be used to assess your essay. If you do not have access to the criteria used in your university, use the examples below.

1   Has the student understood the question?

2   How well does the student know what other scholars have written about the topic?

3   How skilfully has the student evaluated the work of other scholars?

4   To what extent has the student synthesized the information and ideas available to produce a convincing argument?

5   How clearly has that argument been conveyed?

6   Has the student learned what they were supposed to learn from the course?

As you re-read your draft, look for evidence that you have fulfilled each criterion. If you cannot find evidence, make the necessary changes.

The following three exercises will show you how to apply assessment criteria to a sample student essay about internet addiction in Japan.

For more information on assessment criteria, see Chapter 1.

Exercise 1

Read the introductory paragraph of the student's essay written in response to the essay question below. Answer questions 1 and 2.

1   Is the student's interpretation of the research question appropriate? How can you tell?

2   In which part of the paragraph does the writer go off topic?

Write a 1000 word essay discussing the phenomenon of internet addiction within a country or context with which you are familiar. What, in your view, has contributed to the emergence of internet addiction within that context? What, if anything, can be done to address the problem?

Online Communication and Internet Addiction among Young People in Japan

Advances in telecommunications and internet technology have made it possible to exchange information with other users all over the world and at any time. According to Internet World Stats (2012), global use of the internet has increased approximately five fold between 2000 and 2012. In Japan alone, there were just over 100 million users in June, 2012, 79.5 per cent of the population. The top computer manufacturers include IBM, Dell, Hewlett-Packard, and Apple (HubPages, 2012). These companies are very profitable. Apple alone posted profits of £8.8 billion in the three months to July 2012 (Apple, 2012). Although widespread internet access has undoubted advantages, one unintended consequence has been the emergence of internet addiction. The purpose of this essay is to investigate this phenomenon in Japan focussing on young people. The essay is divided into three parts. Firstly, internet addiction is defined. Secondly, the origins of the problem in the Japanese context are discussed. Finally, recommendations are given.

Exercise 2

Read the list of references and the second and third paragraphs of the essay. Consider them in relation to the four questions below.

1   Has the student referred to an acceptable number and range of source materials?

2   What has the student used source material for?

3   How skilfully has the student evaluated the work of other scholars?

4   What could the student have done differently to improve her use of sources?

Reference list

Apple Press Info. (2012). Apple Reports Third Quarter Results. Accessed November 19, 2012. http://apple.com/pr/library/2012/07/24Apple-Reports-Third-Quarter-Results.html.

Greenfield, D.N. (1999). Psychological Characteristics of Compulsive Internet Use: A Preliminary Analysis. *CyberPsychology &Behavior* 2:403–412. Accessed November 20, 2012. doi:10.1089/cpb.1999.2.403.

HubPages. (2012). Computer Companies – Top 10 Computer Manufacturing Companies in the World. Accessed November 19, 2012. http://the-engineer.hubpages.com.

Internet World Stats. 2012. World Internet Usage and Population Statistics. Accessed November 18, 2012. http://www.internetworldstats.com/stats.htm.

Ishii, K. (2003). Internet Use Via Mobile Phone in Japan. *Telecommunications Policy* 28:43–58.

Ito, Mizuko. (2005). Mobile Phones, Japanese Youth, and the Re-placement of Social Contact: Mobile Communications Re-negotiation of the Social Sphere. *Computer Supported Cooperative Work* 31:131–148.

Office for National Statistics. (2009). Internet Access Households and Individuals: Internet Access Statistical Bulletin. Accessed November 21, 2012. http://www.statistics.gov.uk/pdfdir/iahi0809.pdf.

Teo, A.R. and Gaw, A.C. (2010). Hikikomori, a Japanese Culture-Bound Syndrome of Social Withdrawal? *Journal of Nervous and Mental Disease* 198:444–449.

What Japan Thinks. (2009). Two in Five Japanese Ignorant of Public WiFi Networks. Accessed November 22, 2012. http://whatjapanthinks.com/.

Young, K.S. (1998). Internet Addiction: The Emergence of a New Clinical Disorder. *CyberPsychology & Behavior* 1: 237–244. Accessed November 22, 2012. doi:10.1089/cpb.1998.1.237.

Paragraphs 2 and 3

Internet addiction has been defined in various ways. Young (1998), for example, stated that 'Pathological Gambling was viewed as most akin to the pathological nature of internet use. By using Pathological Gambling as a model, addictive internet use can be defined as an impulse-control disorder that does not involve an intoxicant' (Young, 1998, 237). She added that users do not become addicted to the internet itself, rather to particularly addictive applications. Greenfield (1999) stated that it is the speed and accessibility of information that leads to dependence. However, there are other factors specific to Japan which appear to have contributed to the emergence of internet addiction in that context.

The way in which personal communication media developed in Japan encouraged users to acquire the habit of online communication relatively early on. The first cellular phone service in Japan became available in 1979, earlier than in much of the rest of the world. Because the cost of phone calls is high, mobile phones have been and are still mainly used to exchange emails (Ishii, 2003). Another factor driving the use of online communication, particularly among young people, is the lack of physical space. Japanese youth are driven to use mobile phone and internet technology to create a virtual place where they can be independent and free of adult supervision. 'Although a limited form of contact, mobile email has fulfilled a function akin to co-presence for people that lack the means to share the same private physical space' (Ito, 2005, 16). The constant availability of the internet via mobile phones plus the need to use it as a substitute for a shared physical space have encouraged dependence on online communication. However, internet addiction is not a simple phenomenon; it is related to other social problems.

Exercise 3

Now consider the fourth paragraph in relation to the following criterion.

To what extent has the student synthesized the information and ideas available to produce a convincing argument?

One aspect of internet addiction among Japanese youth is the phenomenon of 'internet café refugees'. People who have no fixed accommodation sometimes take refuge in internet cafés which are open 24 hours a day and provide food, drink and access to toilet facilities. Due to the Japanese tendency to associate internet use with privacy, these cafés are designed not as open communal spaces but as a collection of booths and private rooms. This arrangement of space reinforces the problem of internet addiction and the social isolation that comes with it. Another manifestation of internet addiction is referred to as *hikikomori*. The term *hikikomori* has no English equivalent but can be loosely translated as a person who spends all of their time at home online, has no interest in school or work, and suffers from more than one mental disorder or symptom (Ministry of Health, Labour and Welfare Japan, 2003 in Teo and Gaw, 2010). It is sometimes confused with autism, but it is different. Unlike autism, which people are born with, *hikikomori* is social in origin. These two new phenomena, internet café refugees and *hikikomori*, suggest that Japanese youth are particularly vulnerable to becoming addicted to private anonymous online communication and as a result, increasingly isolated socially.

Keeping within your word limit

Lecturers normally specify the required length of your essay, either in terms of pages or, more typically, number of words. They should also tell you how much over or under the word limit you can go. This is normally around 10% either way, but the guidelines can vary, so you should always ask if you are unsure. As you complete each section, it is helpful to check that you are on target to meet your word limit.

Exercise 4

Look again at the parts of the student essay on internet addiction that you have read so far, and in particular at the final section of the introductory paragraph. Answer questions 1–3.

1 How many sections of the paper are there?

2 Approximately what percentage of the 1000 word limit has the student used so far?

3 Assuming that the next paragraph (number five) covers 'recommendations', is the student on target to meet the 1000 word limit?

When students begin writing, they often worry that they will not be able to write enough, particularly if the assignment is longer than they are used to. They may be tempted to 'pad' their writing with extra information and/or unnecessary repetition. In fact, students often discover that the problem is not that they write too little, but that they write too much.

Tips

✓ Write to a plan. Points that are logically organized can usually be expressed in fewer words than points that are loosely organized.

✓ Remove unnecessary repetition. If you have used two or three words to express the same idea, choose one.

✓ Remove material that simply displays knowledge rather than developing the argument.

✓ Reduce descriptive sections. Keep only as much description as is necessary to support the main points in your essay.

✓ Select only key points for in depth analysis. If, for example, you discover that television commercials affect children in six different ways, consider analysing three or four of them.

✓ Mention less important points but state that they will not be covered in detail.

✓ Choose one or two good examples to illustrate a point rather than numerous ordinary examples.

Exercise 5

Read the fifth paragraph of the student's essay and cross out up to 50 words of 'padding'.

It is not easy to imagine completely eradicating internet addiction without eradicating the internet itself. The internet has developed to the point where it is impossible to imagine life without it. The internet is essential and part of daily life for many people. However, there may be ways of lessening the social isolation associated with excessive internet use if we look to what happens in countries outside of Japan. Many countries such as the UK, Germany, France, Canada, the US and Australia have widely available Local Area Network (LAN) hotspots where the public can have free wireless access to the internet via Wireless Fidelity (Wi-Fi). Wi-Fi is a trademark of the Wi-Fi Alliance and it applies to devices that adhere to the Institute of Electrical and Electronics Engineers' standard number 802.11. According to the Office for National Statistics (2009), 2.5 million people in the UK accessed the internet through Wi-Fi in 2009, compared to 700,000 people in 2007. Furthermore, not only public places such as airports or stations but also cafés and restaurants offer free wireless access to the internet. Japan, in contrast, has far less access to and knowledge of public Wi-Fi. In fact, in a recent study, 39.2 per cent of the internet users surveyed said that they were not familiar with public wireless LAN hotspots and 77.3 per cent had never used a public wireless LAN from their laptop (What Japan Thinks, 2009). If free wireless LANs were more available in public places in Japan, people would be more likely to use the internet in public spaces rather than in private study rooms. People might use the internet more carefully because they can be observed publicly. Moreover, they would at least have the opportunity to combine face-to-face social interaction with online interaction, thereby reducing the isolation that is characteristic of internet addiction.

Too few words

If you find it difficult to write enough, this may be because you have not done enough reading or explored your topic in sufficient detail or depth. The easiest remedy may be to add more descriptive detail and examples. However, beware of simply padding a 'thin' essay. Ideally, you should add content that demonstrates higher order thinking skills such as analysis and critical evaluation.

For more information on analysis and critical evaluation, see Chapter 1.

Exercise 6

Do a key word search on Google Scholar™ to find information to add to the paragraph below. Give your own commentary as well.

Parents could also be made aware of the dangers of allowing their children unlimited access to the internet. The warning signs of internet addiction could also be publicized. These measures can reduce the likelihood of the problem becoming worse.

Editing the final draft

Glossary

proofread
When someone proofreads something such as a book or an article, they read it before it is published or submitted in order to find and mark mistakes that need to be corrected.

Before submitting your final draft, it is important to proofread it carefully for errors. Although the content is the most important aspect of your essay, frequent errors can leave a poor impression and make it difficult for the marker to focus on what is good about your essay.

Different university departments often have different policies regarding assistance with proofreading. Some tolerate and even encourage it; others insist that a student's essay must be entirely their own work. Whatever the policy in your university, it is important to develop the ability to recognize and correct errors in your work.

Tips When proofreading:

- ✓ Read your essay aloud slowly.
- ✓ Read a paper copy.
- ✓ Be aware of the types of errors you frequently make and check for these carefully.
- ✓ Look for one type of error at a time.
- ✓ If you are in doubt about the clarity of a sentence, simplify it.
- ✓ Pay particular attention to your references.

Exercise 7

The concluding paragraph of the student's essay contains the errors listed below. Find and correct the errors, making the minimum number of changes necessary.

Sentence 1: word order   Sentence 2: part of speech   Sentence 5: sentence fragment (= a clause or phrase that is punctuated as a sentence but is not a grammatically complete sentence)
Sentence 8: subject-verb agreement   Sentence 10: punctuation

To sum up, this essay has shown how has the internet influenced Japanese youth. Personalization of internet use, which began with the development of mobile phones, encouraged users to become increasing dependent on online communication. Today, the role of the internet in young people's lives is quite complex because it gives them something they need: a separate social space. The emergence of internet café refugees and *hikikomori* indicate that internet addiction is also complex and connected to other social issues such as homelessness and poor mental health. Although it is not possible to know where internet technology will proceed in the future. Most people would probably agree that they would not want to do without it. Attempts to eradicate internet addiction are therefore likely to fail. However, there's possible avenues that can be explored. Making free wireless LANs more widely available could reduce the isolation associated with internet addiction. Secondly, making people more aware of the dangers of internet addiction could reduce it's prevalence.

Preparing to submit your work

It is always a good idea to submit a professional looking document. Check your departmental guidelines for information about presentation. The table below shows the questions you should ask. If you do not have specific guidelines, follow the instructions in the right-hand column.

Questions to ask:	What to do if you haven't got specific instructions from your department:
What information do I need to include on my title page?	Write the title, your name, the name of the programme and course, and the date.
Do I need to include a table of contents?	Include a table of contents if you have used headings and your essay is over ten pages long.
What size and style of font should I use?	Use 12 point Times New Roman.
What spacing should I use?	Use double spacing. Skip a space between paragraphs OR indent the first line of a new paragraph by five spaces.
How wide should my margins be?	Allow one inch margins at the top, bottom and either side.
How should I number the pages?	Number all pages except the title page and table of contents (if you have one) in the top right hand corner.

Exercise 8

What information is missing from the title page below? What other aspect of the presentation might you want to change?

Online Communication and Internet Addiction
Among Young People in Japan

Keiko Satou

Organizational and Social Psychology
PS326 The Social Psychology of Communication

Remember

✔ If you have difficulty getting started, free write a first draft.

✔ If you have difficulty staying on topic, write to an outline and keep your essay question nearby.

✔ Use assessment criteria to revise your first draft.

✔ Keep to your word limit.

✔ If you need to reduce the length of your essay, cut material that is repetitive or displays knowledge rather than furthering the argument.

✔ If you need to increase the length, remember to add material that shows you can analyse and evaluate.

✔ Proofread your work carefully using a variety of techniques.

✔ Find out how you are expected to present your work – hand in a polished professional-looking document.

Reference list

This is a list of the references that the author used while writing the book. Please use these for further reading.

Age UK, (2012). Care in crisis 2012. Retrieved 8 October 2012, from http://www.ageuk.org.uk/get-involved/campaign/poor-quality-care-services-big-q/care-in-crisis-2012-report/.

Amato, P. R. (1983). Helping behaviour in urban and rural environments: Field studies based on a taxonomic organisation of helping episodes. *Journal of personality and Social Psychology, 45,* 571–586.

Apple Press Info (2012). Apple reports third quarter results. Retrieved 22 November 2012, from http://www.apple.com/pr/library/2012/07/24Apple-Reports-Third-Quarter-Results.html.

Australian Psychological Society (2010). The social and psychological impact of online social networking. Retrieved 3 November 2012, from http://www.psychology.org.au/Assets/Files/Social-and-Psychological-Impact-of-Social Networking-Sites.pdf.

Bialystok, E. (2009). Bilingualism: The good, the bad, and the indifferent. *Bilingualism: Language and Cognition, 12(1),* 3–11.

Bryan, J. H., & Test, M. A. (1967). Models and helping: Naturalistic studies in aiding behaviour. *Journal of Personality and Social Psychology, 6(4),* 400–407.doi. 10.1037/h0024826.

Buckley, C. (2011, September 19). China's Sina to step-up censorship of Weibo. Reuters. Retrieved 25 November 2012, from http://in.reuters.com/article/2011/09/19/idINIndia-59420220110919.

Byrne, D. (1971). *The attraction paradigm.* New York: Academic Press.

Chan, K. W., Kwong, C. K., & Dillon, T. S. (2012). *Computational intelligence techniques for new product design.* New York: Springer.

The Chicago manual of Style Online 16th edition (2010). Retrieved 22 November 2012, from http://www.chicagomanualofstyle.org/home.html.

Chou, H. G. & Edge, N. (2012). "They are happier and having better lives than I am": The impact of using Facebook on perceptions of others' lives.

Cyberpsychology, Behavior, and Social Networking, 15(2), 117–121.

Clore, G. L., & Byrne, D. (1974). A reinforcement-affect model of attraction. In T. L. Huston (Ed.), *Foundations of interpersonal attraction* (pp. 143–165). New York: Academic Press.

Clore, G. L. (1976). Interpersonal attraction: An overview. In J. W. Thibaut, J. T. Spence & R. C. Carson (Eds.), *Contemporary topics in social psychology* (pp. 135–175). Morristown, NJ: General Learning Press.

CNNIC (2012). CNNIC released the report on searching behaviour of Chinese netizens. Retrieved 25 November 2012, from http://www1.cnnic.cn/AU/MediaC/rdxw/2012nrd/201208/t20120829_35677.htm.

Crainer, S. & Dearlove, D. (1995). *The Financial Times handbook of management.* Harlow, Essex: Pearson Education.

Cullen, H. (2010). *The Weather of the future: Heat waves, extreme storms, and other scenes from a climate-changed planet.* New York: Harper Collins.

Festinger, L., Schachter, S., & Black, K. (1950). *Social pressures in informal groups: A study of human factors in housing.* New York: Harper.

Foa, E. B., & Foa, U. G. (1975). *Resource theory of social exchange.* Morristown, NJ: General Learning Press.

Glenny, M. (2009). *McMafia: Seriously organised crime.* London: Vintage Books.

Gordon, S., & Ford, R. (2006). On the definition and classification of cybercrime. *Journal of Computer Virology, 2,* 13–20.

Greenfield, D. (1999). Psychological characteristics of compulsive Internet use: A preliminary analysis. *CyberPsychology & Behavior 2,* 403–412. Retrieved 22 November 2012. doi:10.1089/cpb.1999.2.403.

Grosjean, F. (1982). *Life with two languages: An introduction to bilingualism*. Cambridge, MA: Harvard University Press.

Hogg, M. A., & Vaughan, G. M. (2011). *Social psychology 6th edition*. Harlow, Essex: Pearson Education.

HubPages (2012). Computer companies – top 10 computer manufacturing companies in the world. Retrieved 22 November 2012, from http://the-engineer.hubpages.com.

Hunton, P. (2009). The growing phenomenon of crime and the internet: A cybercrime execution and analysis model. *Computer Law & Security Review, 25(6), 528–535.*

Hunton, P. (2011). The stages of cybercrime investigations: Bridging the gap between technology examination and law enforcement investigation. *Computer Law & Security Review, 27(1), 61–67.*

Inceoglu, I., Segers, J., & Bartram, D. (2012). Age-related differences in work motivation. *Journal of Occupational & Organizational Psychology, 85(2), 300–329.*

Internet Crime Complaint Centre (2010). 2010 Internet crime report. Retrieved 15 July 2010, from www.ic3.gov/media/2010/100312.aspx.

Internet Crime Complaints Centre (2012). 2011 Internet crime report. Retrieved 29 October 2012, from http://www.ic3.gov.

Internet World Stats (2012). World Internet usage and population statistics. Retrieved 22 November 2012, from http://www.internetworldstats.com/stats.htm.

Ishii, K. (2003).Internet use via mobile phone in Japan. *Telecommunications Policy, 28, 43–58.*

Islam, G. (2009). Animating leadership: Crisis and renewal of governance in 4 mythic narratives. *The Leadership Quarterly, 20(5), 828–836.*

Ito, M. (2005). Mobile phones, Japanese youth, and the re-placement of social contact: Mobile communications re-negotiation of the social sphere. *Computer Supported Cooperative Work, 31, 131–148.*

Muise, A., Christofides, E., & Desmarais, S. (2009). More information than you ever wanted: Does Facebook bring out the green-eyed monster of jealousy? *CyberPsychology & Behavior, 12(4), 441–444.* doi:10.1089/cpb.2008.0263.

Mullins, L. J. (2010). *Management and organisational behaviour*. Harlow, Essex: Pearson Education.

Newcomb, T. M. (1961). *The acquaintance process*. New York: Holt, Rinehart & Winston.

Office of Fair Trading (2009). The psychology of scams: Provoking and committing errors of judgement. Retrieved 1 November 2012, from http://www.oft.gov.uk/shared_oft/reports/consumer_protection/oft1070.pdf.

Office for National Statistics (2009). Internet access households and individuals: Internet access statistical bulletin – 2009. Retrieved 22 November 2012, from www.statistics.gov.uk/pdfdir/iahi0809.pdf.

Portnoy, M., & Goodman, S. (2009). A brief history of global responses to cyber threats. In M. Portnoy & S. Goodman (Eds.), *Global initiatives to secure cyberspace: An emerging landscape* (pp. 1–6). New York: Springer.

Przybyla, D. P. J. (1985). *The facilitating effects of exposure to erotica on male prosocial behaviour*. Unpublished doctoral dissertation, State University of New York at Albany.

Rusbult, C. E., Martz, J.M., & Agnew, C. R. (1998). The Investment Model Scale: Measuring commitment level, satisfaction level, quality of alternatives, and investment size. *Personal Relationships, 5, 357–391.*

Semanza, J. C. (2003). The intersection of urban planning, art, and public health: The Sunnyside Piazza. *American Journal of Public Health, 93(9), 1439–1441.*

Simonton, D. K. (2008). Bilingualism and creativity. In J. Altarriba & R. R. Heredia (Eds.), *An introduction to bilingualism: Principles and processes* (pp. 147–166). Mahwah, NJ: Lawrence Erlbaum.

Small, G., & Vorgan, G. (2008). *iBrain: Surviving the technological alteration of the modern mind*. New York: Collins Living.

Smith, R.G., Grabosky, P. and Urbas, G. (2004)

Cyber criminals on trial, Cambridge: Cambridge University Press.

Tannenbaum, R. & Schmidt, W. H. (1973). How to choose a leadership pattern. *Harvard Business Review, 73311,* 3–12.

Teo, A. & Gaw A. (2010). Hikikomori, a Japanese culture-bound syndrome of social withdrawal? *Journal of Nervous and Mental Disease, 198,* 444–449.

Thibaut, J. W., & Kelley, H. H. (1959). *The social psychology of groups.* New York: Wiley.

Tucker, G. R. (1999). A Global perspective on bilingualism and bilingual education. Center for Applied Linguistics. Retrieved 10 August 2012, from http://www.cal.org/resources/digest/digestglobal.html.

Twitter (2012, March 21). Twitter turns six. Retrieved 25 November 2012, from http://blog.twitter.com/2012/03/twitter-turns-six.html.

UK Cards Association (2010). Plastic fraud figures. Retrieved 14 July 2010, from http://www.theukcardsassociation.org.uk/plastic_fraud_figures/index.asp.

Wall, D.S. (2005). The Internet as a conduit for criminals. In Pattavina (Ed.) *Information technology and the criminal justice system* (pp. 77–98). Thousand Oaks, CA: SAGE. Retrieved 14 July 2010, from http://papers.ssrn.com/sol3/papers.cfm?abstract_id=740626.

Wall, D.S. (2008). Cybercrime, media and insecurity. *International Review of Law Computers and Technology, 22(1),* 45–63.

Warneken, F. & Tomasello, M. (2006). Altruistic helping in human infants and young chimpanzees. *Science, 311 (5765),* 1301–1303.

What Japan Thinks (2009). Two in five Japanese ignorant of public WiFi networks. Retrieved 22 November 2012, from http://whatjapanthinks.com.

Wodzicki, K., Schwämmlein, E., & Moskaliuk, J. (2012). "Actually, I wanted to learn": Study-related knowledge exchange on social networking sites. *The Internet and Higher Education, 15(1),* 9–14.

Young, K. (1998). Internet addiction: The emergence of a new clinical disorder. *CyberPsychology & Behavior 1,* 237–244. Retrieved 22 November 2012. doi:10.1089/cpb.1998.1.237.

Zimski, P. (2011). Navigating the new threat landscape. *Computer Law & Security Review, 2011(5),* 5–8.

Appendix 1 — Critical reading checklist

Critical analysis is a complex skill which involves looking at many aspects of the text you are interested in. It is easy to be persuaded by a text that appears to be authoritative. To help you maintain an objective critical stance and perform a thorough analysis, use the following questions as a guide. Sections 1–5 can be applied to most academic texts. If you are evaluating an empirical study or report, Sections 6 and 7 are also very important.

1   Author(s)

   a   What are the author's credentials?

   b   Is the author affiliated to a reputable organization?

2   Publication

   a   Who funded the research and is there the possibility of bias? Would the author gain financially from presenting the content in a certain way?

   b   Has the text been published by a recognized publisher, journal or organization?

   c   Has it been peer-reviewed?

   d   When was it published? Is it sufficiently up-to-date?

3   Language

   a   Is the author's use of language appropriate to his/her research?

   b   Is it persuasive?

   c   Is it clear and precise?

   d   Is it professional?

   e   Is it objective?

4   Argument

   a   What is the context it applies to? Is the context sufficiently related to the context of your essay for its findings to be relevant?

   b   What question or issue is it exploring?

   c   Does the author provide an adequate rationale for her/his choice of question?

   d   What is the author's theoretical approach?

   e   What is the author's position on the question or issue?

   f   What is the author's argument?

   g   What evidence does the author offer in support of her/his argument?

5   Research review

   a   Does the author cover an adequate range of research?

   b   Are there any significant omissions?

   c   Does the author show bias, for example, by quoting his/her own previous research extensively?

6 Conclusion

   a Do the conclusions follow from the evidence presented?

   b Are alternative conclusions discussed?

   c Does the author adequately answer the original question?

7 Methodology

   a Why was the method chosen?

   b Is the methodology capable of answering the question?

   c Was the method tested/piloted?

   d Are any alternative methods discussed?

   e Are any biases or difficulties with the method discussed?

8 Findings

   a Are the findings significant? Do they tell us something we didn't know before?

   b Are a range of reasons for any significant findings evaluated?

   c Are the findings compared to findings of similar research? Are any significant differences adequately explained?

Source: Adapted from material supplied by Esther Daborn, University of Glasgow, April 2008.

Appendix 2 — Instruction words

The following words are commonly used in essay questions or instructions. They will also be useful to you when you are writing up your essay. You can use them to describe the different parts of your essay (you normally do this towards the end of your introductory section) and for reporting the views of other scholars. Study the definitions and examples given below.

Instruction word	Definition	Examples
account for	Explain why something happened or why something is the way it is	Account for the success of the co-operative movement in nineteenth century Britain.
		This essay traces the emergence of the cooperative movement and accounts for its success in nineteenth century Britain.
clarify	Make something clearer or easier to understand by explaining it or simplifying it	Clarify the role of human resource manager.
		Smith (1987) clarifies the role of human resource manager.
define	Give the meaning of a term or concept; discuss problems with defining the term and alternative definitions	Define the term 'political correctness'.
		The Oxford English dictionary defines 'political correctness' as 'the avoidance of forms of expression or action that are perceived to exclude, marginalize, or insult groups of people who are socially disadvantaged or discriminated against'.
demonstrate	Show how something can, is, or should be done, or show clearly that something is true by giving proof	Demonstrate the correlation between vocabulary acquisition and reading speed.
		The final part of this study demonstrates the correlation between vocabulary acquisition and reading speed.
distinguish	Explain the differences between two or more things	Distinguish between depredation by polar bears and that of other arctic predators.
		This essay shows how depredation by polar bears can be distinguished from that of other arctic predators.
elaborate	Give more detailed information and/or explanation of something	Elaborate on the poet's relationship with his father, alluded to indirectly in the second verse.
		In his 2007 study, Carter elaborates on the poet's relationship with his father.
elucidate	Explain or make something clear	Elucidate the mechanism by which statins reduce rates of LDL cholesterol in the blood.
		A number of studies published in the 1990s elucidated the mechanism by which statins reduce rates of LDL cholesterol in the blood (Myers et al. 1994, Hume et al. 1996).

enumerate	List the relevant points or information	Enumerate the demands made by striking miners during the 1984 industrial dispute.
		Jones (2003) enumerates the demands made by striking miners and shows how these were systematically misreported in televised news broadcasts at the time.
explore	Use a questioning approach to consider something from a variety of points of view	Explore the representation of children in eighteenth century cautionary tales.
		This essay explores the representation of children in eighteenth century cautionary tales.
interpret	Make the underlying meaning of something explicit	Interpret Orwell's parable *Animal Farm* in light of the changing political climate of his day.
		McGregor (2001) interprets Orwell's *Animal Farm* in light of the changing political climate of his day.
review	Critically evaluate something or a series of related things	Review the literature on corporations' financial performance and commitment to ethics.
		This essay begins by reviewing the literature on corporations' financial performance and commitment to ethics.
summarize	Give a condensed version of something focussing on the main points	Summarize Belton's views on the relationship between boredom and creativity.
		Philips (2009) summarizes Belton's views on creativity and boredom and offers his own alternative interpretation.
to what extent	Evaluate the evidence for and against something (NB this expression implies that there is probably no clear cut answer)	To what extent does exam stress contribute to low mood in adolescence?
		This essay assesses the extent to which exam stress contributes to low mood among adolescents.

Appendix 3 — Prefixes, suffixes and roots

A prefix is a letter or a group of letters, for example 'un-' or 'multi-', which is added to the beginning of a word (or 'root') in order to form a different word. A suffix is a letter or a group of letters, for example '-ly' or '-ness', which is added to the end of a word in order to form a different word, often of a different word class. Recognizing prefixes, suffixes and roots can help you work out the meaning of unfamiliar words. The table below lists some of the most common prefixes, suffixes and roots in English. Those marked with a * are particularly common in academic English.

Prefixes		
a-, ad-	to, towards, near	aside = (adv) to one side; adhere = (verb) to stick to
a-, an-	not, without	apolitical = (adj) without a political view; anaerobic = (adj) without oxygen from the air
ab-	away from	abstain = (verb) to avoid doing something that is enjoyable but possibly wrong or unhealthy
ambi-	both	ambiguous = (adj) can be understood in more than one way; unclear
ante-	before	antecedent = (noun) something that happened before something else
anti-	against, opposite	antisocial = (adj) against social norms
auto-	self	autonomous = (adj) independent; able to make your own decisions
bene-	good	beneficial = (adj) having a good effect
bi-	two	biannual = (adj) happening twice every year
bio-	life	biography = (noun) an account of someone's life
circum-	around	circumvent = (verb) to go around an obstacle or limitation
*co-, com-, con-	with, together	co-owner = (noun) someone who owns something with another person; compatible = (adj) able to exist or work together; converge = (verb) to join from different directions
com-, con-	complete	complete = (adj) containing all the parts or features; confirmation = (noun) a statement that something is definitely true
contra-, counter-	opposite, against	contravene = (verb) to do something that is against a law or agreement; counterintuitive = (adj) opposite to what seems normal or natural
cyber-	computer	cybercrime = (noun) computer crime
de-	from, away, opposite	devolve = (verb) to take power from a central authority
di-, du-	two, twice	diverge = (verb) to begin to go in separate directions; duplicate = (verb) to repeat or copy something

dia-	through, across	diaspora = (noun) a group of people originating in one place but now living in many different parts of the world
*dis-	not, opposite, away	dispute = (verb) to say that something is not true
dys-	bad, abnormal	dysfunctional = (adj) functioning badly
e-	away, out	eject = (verb) to force someone or something out
e-	internet related	e-commerce = (noun) trade via the internet
eco-	ecology or economy related	eco-friendly = (adj) designed to cause minimum harm to the environment; economize = (verb) to use carefully to avoid waste
em-, en-	make, provide with	empower = (verb) to give someone more power; enable = (verb) to make someone able to do something
ex-	out, former	exposed = (adj) not covered or hidden; ex-wife = former wife
exter-, extra-	outside, beyond	external = (adj) coming from outside; extraneous = (adj) not relevant to the subject being considered
fore-	before	foresight = (noun) the ability to see what is likely to happen in the future
geo-	earth	geology = (noun) the study of the Earth's structure, surface and origins
hyper-	above, over	hyperinflation = (noun) very severe inflation
il-, im-, in-, ir-	not	illegible = (adj) not clear enough to be read; immature (adj) not mature; inaccurate = (adj) not accurate; irresponsible = (adj) not behaving in a responsible way
inter-	between	international = (adj) between or involving different countries
intra-	inside, within	intranet = (noun) a network of computers within a particular company or organization
kilo-	thousand	kilometre = (noun) a thousand metres
macro-	big	macroeconomics = (noun) the branch of economics dealing with the major features of the economy
mal-	bad	malfunction = (verb) to fail to work properly
mega-	great, million	megawatt = (noun) a million watts
micro-	small	microbiology = (noun) the branch of biology concerned with the study of very small living things such as bacteria
mid-	middle	midpoint = (noun) the point that divides something into two halves
mill-	thousand	millennium = (noun) a period of one thousand years
mini-	small	mini-market = (noun) a small market
*mis-	wrongly	misinterpret = (verb) to interpret something incorrectly
mono-	one	monograph = (noun) a detailed study of only one subject

multi-	many	multicultural = (adj) relating to people from many different cultures and nationalities
neo-	new	neologism = (noun) a new word or expression
non-	not	non-fiction = (noun) writing that gives factual information rather than telling a story
*out-	more, better than	out-perform = (verb) to perform better than another
*over-	excessive, above	overstatement = (noun) an exaggeration
poly-	many	polygamy = (noun) the custom of allowing marriage to more than one person at the same time
post-	after	postgraduate = (adj) after a first degree
pre-	before	prearrange = (verb) to arrange ahead of time
pro-	in support of	pro-democracy = (adj) in support of democracy
proto-	first	prototype = (noun) the first or preliminary model of something
pseudo-	false	pseudo-democracy = (noun) not really a democracy
*re-	back, again	revise = (verb) to work on something again to improve or adjust it
retro-	backwards	retrospective = (adj) looking back on past events
semi-	half, partly	semiconscious = (adj) partly conscious or aware
*sub-	under; part of; inferior	submerge = (verb) to go under water; subcommittee = (noun) a committee which is part of a larger committee; substandard = (adj) below the required standard
super-	higher, more than	supercomputer = (noun) a powerful computer able to process large amounts of data very quickly
sur-	above	surcharge = (noun) an extra payment
trans-	across	transition = (noun) the process of changing from one state to another
tri-	three	trilogy = (noun) a series of three related books, plays or films
ultra-	beyond, to an extreme degree	ultra-modern = (adj) very modern
*un-	not; reverse an action	unarguable = (adj) so correct that it is not open to discussion; unwrap = (verb) to remove the covering from something
under-	not enough	underprivileged = (adj) having insufficient money or opportunities

Suffixes		
-able, -ible	(adj) worth, able	readable = (adj) able to be read; credible = (adj) worthy of trust or belief
-acy, -cy	(noun) state, quality	supremacy = (noun) the state of being better or more powerful; privacy = (noun) the state of being free from the attention of others
*-age	(noun) state, related to	marriage = (noun) the state of being married

-al	(noun) action, result of action	referral = (noun) the act of officially sending someone to a person qualified to help them
*-al, -ial, -ical	(adj) relating to	structural = (adj) relating to the structure of something; glacial = (adj) relating to a glacier, icy; farcical = (adj) extremely ridiculous, like a farce
-an	(noun) person who does something	historian = (noun) a person who studies history
-ance, -ence	(noun) action, state, quality	tolerance = (noun) the quality of allowing other people to do as they like; independence = (noun) the state of being independent
-ancy, -ency	(noun) state, quality	vacancy = (noun) the state of being vacant or empty; dependency = (noun) the state of being dependent
*-ant, -ent	(noun) someone or something that does or has something	occupant = (noun) someone who occupies something; agent = (noun) a person who does business on someone else's behalf
-arian	(adj) believing in, having	humanitarian = (adj) seeking to promote human welfare
-ate	(adj) filled with	compassionate = (adj) filled with compassion
*-ate	(verb) cause to be	complicate = (verb) to make something more difficult to deal with
-ation	(noun) state of	dehydration = (noun) the state when your body does not have enough water
-cle, cule	(adj, noun) small	particle = (noun) a very small piece or amount of something; minuscule = (adj) very small
-dom	(noun) state of being	freedom = (noun) the state of being free
-ed	(adj) having the quality of	moneyed = (adj) having money
-ee	(noun) person who receives something	payee = (noun) the person who receives pay
-en	(adj) material	wooden = (adj) made of wood
*-en	(verb) cause, make	shorten = (verb) to make shorter
*-ent	(adj) being in a state or condition	dependent = (adj) needing someone or something
*-er, -eer, -eur -or	(noun) person who does something	astronomer = (noun) a scientist who studies stars, planets and other objects in space; volunteer = (noun) a person who works without being paid for it; entrepreneur = (noun) a person who sets up a business; author = (noun) a person who writes books
*-ery	(noun) place where something happens; instance of something happening	bakery = (noun) a place where bread, cakes and similar things are baked and/or sold; bribery = (noun) the act of offering someone a bribe

-ess	(noun) female	actress = (noun) a woman whose job is to act in plays or films
-ette	(noun) small	statuette = (noun) a small statue
-free	(adj) without	carefree = (adj) without problems or responsibilities
*-ful	(adj) filled with	careful = (adj) doing things with care and attention
-hood	(noun) state, condition	adulthood = (noun) the state of being an adult
-ician	(noun) person who works at something	dietician = (noun) a person whose job is to give advice about what to eat
-ics	(noun) system, knowledge of	ethics = (noun) moral beliefs and rules about right and wrong
*-ify	(verb) make	intensify = (verb) to make something more intense
*-ise, -ize	(verb) make	normalise = (verb) to make something normal or to become normal
*-ism	(noun) action, state, belief	optimism = (noun) a feeling of being hopeful about the future
-ist	(noun) someone who practises	pharmacist = (noun) a person qualified to prepare and sell medicines
*-ity	(noun) state	simplicity = (noun) the state of being simple
*-ive	(adj) having the quality of	cooperative = (adj) involving working together
*-less	(adj) without	boundless = (adj) without boundaries or limits
-let	(noun) little	droplet = (noun) a little drop of liquid
-like	(adj) similar	birdlike = (adj) moving or looking like a bird
-logy, -ology	(noun) study of	anthropology = (noun) the scientific study of people, society and culture
-ly	(adv) in the manner of	easily = (adv) with ease
*-ment	(noun) state, condition	management = (noun) the control and organizing of a business or other organization
-mony	(noun) resulting state	testimony = (noun) a formal written or spoken statement, especially in a court of law
*-ness	(noun) state	awareness = (noun) the state of being aware of or knowing about something
-oid	(adj, noun) resembling	android = (noun) a robot that looks like a human being
-ory	(adj, noun) place where something happens; relating to	depository = (noun) a place where things can be stored; advisory = (adj) having the role of giving advice, making suggestions
-otic	(adj) affecting, causing	patriotic = (adj) inspiring love of your own country
*-ous	(adj) having the qualities of	dangerous = (adj) likely to harm
*-ship	(noun) condition, state	censorship = (noun) the suppression of communication considered dangerous or offensive

*-sion, -tion	(noun) instance or act of doing something	invasion = (noun) the act of invading a place; inspection = (noun) the act of inspecting something
-some	(adj) causing	troublesome = (adj) causing trouble or difficulty
-ty	(noun) state or quality	lucidity = (noun) the state of being lucid or clear
-ulent	(adj) full of	opulent = (adj) grand and expensive, full of riches
-ure	(noun) act, condition	exposure = (noun) the act of exposing or putting into contact with; the state of being exposed
-ward	(adv) in the direction of	inward = (adv) directed or moving toward the inside
-wide	(adj, adv) extending throughout	worldwide = (adj) extending throughout the world
-wise	(adv) in the direction or manner of	likewise = (adv) similarly, in the same way
-worthy	deserving	praiseworthy = (adj) deserving of praise

Roots		
act, ag	do, act, go	action = (noun) the process of doing something; agenda = (noun) the things that need to be done or discussed
ali, alter	other, different	alien = (adj) from a different country, race or culture; alteration = (noun) a change in form or appearance
ann, enn	yearly	annual = (adj) occurring yearly; biennial = (adj) occurring once every two years
auc, aug	increase	auction = (noun) a public sale where things are sold to the person who offers the highest price; augment = (verb) to increase the amount or size of something
aud	hear	audible = (adj) loud enough to be heard
bibl	book	bibliography = (noun) a list of books and other publications used in a piece of work or related to a particular topic
brev	short	abbreviate = (verb) to make a word or piece of writing shorter
cap	seize	captivating = (adj) attracting attention, fascinating
cent	hundred	century = (noun) one hundred years
cert	true	ascertain = (verb) to find out the truth about something
chron	time	chronicle = (noun) a record of events that happened in the past
civ	citizen	civilization = (noun) a society with its own culture
clar	clear	clarify = (verb) to make something clear or easier to understand
claus, clud, clus	close	clause = (noun) a separate part of a bill, contract or treaty; exclude = (verb) to shut out; inclusive = (adj) = taking in everything within its scope
cosm	universe, world	microcosm = (noun) a small world or society with the features of a larger one
cracy	rule	democracy = (noun) rule by the people

cred	believe	credible = (adj) believable
crit	judge	critique = (noun) an evaluation of something, e.g. someone's work or idea
cur	caring	curator = (noun) a person responsible for looking after objects in a museum
dec	ten	decade = (noun) ten years
dei, div	God, god	deity = (noun) a god; divine = (adj) relating to a god or goddess
del	destroy	delete = (verb) to cross out or remove something that has been written
dem	people	demography = (noun) the study of populations
dict	say	diction = (noun) pronunciation
doct	teach	indoctrinate = (verb) to teach a particular set of beliefs
dom, domin	rule, master	predominant = (adj) more important or noticeable than others
don	give	donate = (verb) to give money or goods, usually to a charity or for a good cause
dox	opinion	orthodox = (adj) accepted by most people, adhering to traditional opinion
epi	near, after	epilogue = (noun) extra comment at the end of a written work
equi	equal	equitable = (adj) fair
fac, fic	make	factory = (noun) a large building where machines are used to mass produce things; artificial = (adj) made by humans, produced rather than natural
fem	female	effeminate = (adj) showing characteristics associated with a woman, unmanly
fend	strike	offend = (verb) to say or do something that upsets others
fer	carry	transfer = (verb) to go or take something from one place to another
fid	faith, trust	confidential = (adj) intended to be kept private
fig	form, shape	disfigure = (verb) to spoil the appearance of something
fin	end	finalize = (verb) to complete something
flex	bending	flexible = (adj) able to bend easily without breaking, adaptable
flict	strike	affliction = (noun) something which causes suffering
flu	flow	influx = (noun) the arrival of a large number of people or things
fort	strong	fortify = (verb) to make something stronger
gen	birth, race, produce	generate = (verb) to produce something
gram	writing, drawing	diagram = (noun) a line drawing used to illustrate how something is constructed or works
graph	writing, drawing	biography = (noun) an account of someone's life

gyn	female, woman	misogynistic = (adj) involving a strong dislike of women
her, hes	stick	adhere = (verb) to stick to; cohesion = (noun) the action of sticking together or forming a whole
hetero	other	heterogeneous = (adj) consisting of elements that are different
hol	whole	holistic = (adj) emphasizing the importance of the whole
homo	same	homogeneous = (adj) consisting of elements that are the same
ide, ideo	idea	ideology = (noun) a set of beliefs, especially political, on which people base their actions
jec	throw	reject = (verb) to refuse to accept something
labor	work	collaborate = (verb) to work together
leg	legal	legislate = (verb) to create a new law
liber	free	liberal = (adj) believing people should have a lot of freedom to decide how to behave and think
lingu	language	linguistics = (noun) the study of the way in which language works
liter	letter	literal = (adj) in accordance with the most basic or exact meaning of a word or words, not metaphorical or figurative
loc, loqu	speak	eloquent = (adj) well expressed
log	reason, speech	dialogue = (noun) discussion or conversation between people
luc, lumin	light	lucid = (adj) expressed clearly, easily understood; luminary = (noun) an expert in a particular subject
magn	great	magnify = (verb) to make an object appear larger
manu	hand	manual = (adj) done by hand
mascul	man	masculinity = (noun) maleness, qualities associated with being a man
mater	mother	maternal = (adj) appropriate to or relating to a mother
maxim	greatest	maximize = (verb) to make something as great as you can
mem	remember	memoir(s) = (noun) a written account of your memories
ment	mind	mental = (adj) relating to the mind or process of thinking
meta	beyond, change	metamorphosis = (noun) complete change or transformation
migr	moving, changing	migrant = (noun) a person who moves from one place to another, especially to find work
min	small, less	diminish = (verb) to become smaller in size, importance or intensity
misc	mix	miscellaneous = (adj) consisting of a variety of different parts that are difficult to categorize
morph	shape	amorphous = (adj) without a clear shape
mut	change	mutate = (verb) to develop different characteristics due to genetic changes
nat	being born	innate = (adj) existing from birth

nom, nym	name	nominate = (verb) to choose someone for a position; antonym = (noun) a word with the opposite meaning to another word
nov	new	innovate = (verb) to introduce new ways of making or doing something
numer	number	enumerate = (verb) to name the items in a list one by one
omni	all	omnipresent = (adj) apparently present everywhere or always
oper	work	co-operate = (verb) to work together for a particular purpose
opt	choose	option = (noun) something that you can choose to do
optim	the best	optimize = (verb) to get the most out of something
pan	all	pan-African = (adj) relating to or involving all of Africa
para	beside	paraphrase = (verb) to express what someone has said or written in a different way
pass, path	feeling	passionate = (adj) having strong feelings about something; empathy = (noun) the ability to share another person's feelings as if they were your own
pater	father	paternal = (adj) appropriate to or relating to a father
pel	force, drive	compel = (verb) to force someone to do something
per	through, thoroughly	perpetual = (adj) never ending or changing
peri	around	perimeter = (noun) the outer edges or boundary around an area
phil	love	Anglophile = (adj) loving British culture or people; philanthropy = (noun) charitable giving
phob	fear	claustrophobia = (noun) fear of enclosed spaces
phon	sound	phonetics = (noun) the study of speech sounds
physic	of nature	physical = (adj) related to the body rather than the mind
plac	please	complacent = (adj) feeling too pleased with oneself
plen	full	replenish = (verb) to make something full again
plur	more	pluralist = (adj) allowing many different groups to co-exist
poli	city	metropolitan = (adj) belonging to or typical of a large city
popul	people	populous = (adj) having a lot of people living in it
pon, pos	put, place	postpone = (verb) to arrange for something to happen later than planned; repository = (noun) a place where something is kept safely
port	carry	portable = (adj) able to be easily carried
pot	power	potent = (adj) powerful
prim, prin	first	primary = (adj) first, most important; principal = (adj) most important
pro	in front of, before	propel = (verb) to push something

proxim	near	proximity = (noun) nearness in space or time
psych	mind	psychology = (noun) the scientific study of the human mind
puls	drive, push	impulse = (noun) a sudden desire to do something
put	think	dispute = (noun) a disagreement
rect	right, straight	rectify = (verb) to make something right
rupt	break	disrupt = (verb) to prevent something from continuing to happen by causing a disturbance
sat	enough	saturate = (verb) to fill something completely
scal	ladder, stairs	escalate = (verb) to increase in size, intensity or seriousness
sci	know	omniscient = (adj) apparently knowing everything
scope	look	microscope = (noun) a scientific instrument that allows you to see very small things
script	writing	manuscript = (noun) a handwritten or typed document, usually the first version of a book before it is published
sect	cut	dissect = (verb) to cut up a dead body to examine it scientifically
secu, sequ, sue	follow	prosecute = (verb) to take legal action against someone; sequence = (noun) a particular order in which things happen or are arranged; pursue = (verb) to follow someone or something with the intention to catch them
sed, sid	sit, stay	sedentary = (adj) sitting too much, inactive; residue = (noun) a small amount of something that remains after most of it has gone
sens, sent	feel, think	sensation = (noun) a physical feeling; consent = (verb) to agree to something
simil, simul	similar	facsimile = (noun) a copy or imitation of something; simultaneous = (adj) happening at the same time
spec, spic	look, see	inspect = (verb) look at something carefully; conspicuous = (adj) easily seen, obvious
stab	steady	stabilize = (verb) to become steady
struct	build	constructive = (adj) useful or helpful
sume, sump	take	consume = (verb) to use a supply of something; presumption = (noun) something that you accept as true but it may not be true
tact, tang	touch	contact = (noun) physical touch, communication; tangible = (adj) perceptible by touch
tech	art, skill	technician = (noun) someone whose job involves skilled practical work with equipment
tele	distance	telescope = (noun) an instrument that makes things in the distance appear larger
tempo	time	contemporary = (adj) living or happening at the same time, related to the present time

tain, ten	hold	detain = (verb) to hold someone back; tenacious = (adj) holding on, not giving up
term	limit, end	terminate = (verb) to end something completely
terr	earth	territory = (noun) an area of land, region
tor	twist	distort = (verb) to twist out of shape, or to give a false account of something
tract	pull	retract = (verb) to pull back, or to withdraw a statement because it is unjustified
trib	pay, give	contribute = (verb) to give money or help in order to achieve something
trude	push	intruder = (noun) a person who goes into a place they are not supposed to be
ultim, ultra	end, last	ultimatum = (noun) a final warning or demand; ultra-rich = (adj) very rich
uni	one	uniform = (adj) not varied, regular throughout
urb	city	urban = (adj) relating to a city
vac	empty	evacuate = (verb) to remove someone from a dangerous place to a safe place
ven	come	convene = (verb) to assemble, or to call people to a meeting
ver	true	verify = (verb) to confirm that something is true
verb	word	verbalize = (verb) to express something
verg, vers, vert	turning	diverge = (verb) to separate or develop in different directions; diversion = (noun) something that turns your attention away from what you are doing; invert = (verb) to turn something the other way up or back to front
vict, vinc	conquer, win	conviction = (noun) a strong belief or opinion; invincible = (adj) impossible to defeat
vid, vis	see	video = (noun) film recorded on tape; visible = (adj) able to be seen
vita	life	vitality = (noun) the state of being strong and lively
viv	live	revive = (verb) to become active, popular or successful again
voc	speak	advocate = (verb) to speak in favour of something
vol	will	benevolent = (adj) kind, wishing others well
with	against, away	withhold = (verb) to keep something away from someone who wants it

Glossary

Some of the more difficult words from the chapters are defined here in this Glossary. The definitions focus on the meanings of the words in the context in which they appear in the text. Definitions are from *COBUILD Advanced Dictionary*.

Key

ABBREVIATION	abbreviation	N-UNCOUNT	uncount noun
ADJ	adjective	N-VAR	variable noun
ADV	adverb	NEG	negative
AUX	auxiliary verb	NUM	number
COLOUR	colour word	ORD	ordinal
COMB	combining form	PASSIVE	see V-PASSIVE
CONJ	conjunction	PHRASAL VERB	phrasal verb
CONVENTION	convention	PHRASE	phrase
DET	determiner	PREDET	predeterminer
EXCLAM	exclamation	PREFIX	prefix
FRACTION	fraction	PREP	preposition
LINK	see V-LINK	PRON	pronoun
MODAL	modal verb	QUANT	quantifier
N-COUNT	count noun	QUEST	question word
N-PLURAL	plural noun	SUFFIX	suffix
N-PROPER	proper noun	VERB	verb
N-PROPER-PLURAL	plural proper noun	V-LINK	link verb
N-SING	singular noun	V-PASSIVE	passive verb
N-TITLE	title noun		

a

abbreviation (abbreviations) N-COUNT
An abbreviation is a short form of a word or phrase, made by leaving out some of the letters or by using only the first letter of each word.

access (accesses, accessing, accessed) VERB
If you access something, you succeed in finding it or obtaining it.

accomplish (accomplishes, accomplishing, accomplished) VERB
If you accomplish something, you succeed in doing it.

adversely ADV
If something adversely affects you, it is unfavourable to you.

advocate (advocates, advocating, advocated) VERB
If you advocate a particular action or plan, you recommend it publicly.

aftermath N-SING
The aftermath of an important event , especially a harmful one, is the situation that results from it.

alphabetically ADV
If something is arranged alphabetically, it is arranged according to the normal order of the letters in the alphabet.

ambiguous ADJ
If you describe something as ambiguous, you mean that it is unclear or confusing because it can be understood in more than one way.

anecdotal evidence N-UNCOUNT
Anecdotal evidence is based on individual accounts, rather than on reliable research or statistics, and so may not be valid.

annotate (annotates, annotating, annotated) VERB
If you annotate written work or a diagram, you add notes to it, especially in order to explain it.

anticipate (anticipates, anticipating, anticipated) VERB
If you anticipate an event, you realize in advance that it may happen and you are prepared for it.

assumption (assumptions) N-COUNT
If you make an assumption that something is true or will happen, you accept that it is true or will happen, often without any real proof.

attitude (attitudes) N-VAR
Your attitude to something is the way that you think and feel about it, especially when this shows in the way you behave.

attribute (attributes, attributing, attributed) VERB
If you attribute something to an event or situation, you think that it was caused by that event or situation.

b

background knowledge N-UNCOUNT
Background knowledge about a topic is information about it that helps explain what caused it or why it is how it is.

bias (biases) N-VAR
Bias is a tendency to prefer one person or thing to another, and to favour that person or thing.

biased ADJ
If someone is biased, they prefer one group of people to another, and behave unfairly as a result.

boundaries N-PLURAL
The boundaries of something such as a subject or activity are the limits that people think that it has.

broadly categorized ADJ
You use broadly categorized to say that something can generally be divided into or be said to belong to particular sets or types.

bulletin (bulletins) N-COUNT
A bulletin is a short official announcement made publicly to inform people about an important matter.

c

chronological ADJ
If things are described or shown in chronological order, they are described or shown in the order in which they happened.

cite (cites, citing, cited) VERB
If you cite something, you quote it or mention it, especially as an example or proof of what you are saying.

commentary (commentaries) N-COUNT
A commentary is an article or book which explains or discusses something.

commission (commissions, commissioning, commissioned) VERB
If you commission something or commission someone to do something, you formally arrange for someone to do a piece of work for you.

complex sentence (complex sentences) N-COUNT
A complex sentence contains one or more subordinate clauses as well as a main clause.

components N-PLURAL
The components of something are the parts that it is made of.

concise ADJ
Something that is concise says everything that is necessary without using any unnecessary words.

concrete ADJ
You use concrete to indicate that something is definite and specific.

condensed ADJ
A condensed book, explanation, or piece of information has been made shorter, usually by including only the most important parts.

confound (confounds, confounding, confounded) VERB
Something that confounds the results of a study confuses or distorts them.

confounding variable (confounding variables) N-COUNT
A confounding variable is an extra factor that can change and distort the results of an experiment or piece of research.

consistent ADJ
Someone who is consistent always behaves in the same way, has the same attitudes towards people and things, or achieves the same level of success in something.

context (contexts) N-VAR
The context of an idea or piece of research is the general situation that relates to it, and which helps it to be understood.

continuum (continua or continuums) N-COUNT [usu sing]
A continuum is a set of things on a scale, which have a particular characteristic to different degrees.

controversial ADJ
If you describe something or someone as controversial, you mean that they are the subject of intense public argument, disagreement, or disapproval.

convey (conveys, conveying, conveyed) VERB
To convey information or feelings means to cause them to be known or understood by someone.

convincing ADJ
If you describe someone or something as convincing, you mean that they make you believe that a particular thing is true, correct, or genuine.

copyright (copyrights) N-VAR
If someone has copyright on a piece of writing or music, it is illegal to reproduce or perform it without their permission.

corroborate (corroborates, corroborating, corroborated) VERB
To corroborate something that has been said or reported means to provide evidence or information that supports it.

credentials N-PLURAL
Someone's credentials are their previous achievements, training, and general background, which indicate that they are qualified to do something.

credible ADJ
Credible means able to be trusted or believed.

d

database (databases) N-COUNT
A database is a collection of data that is stored in a computer and that can be easily used and added to.

debate (debates) N-VAR
A debate is a discussion about a subject on which people have different views.

deduce (deduces, deducing, deduced) VERB
If you deduce something, you reach that conclusion because of other things that you know to be true.

deliberate ADJ
If you do something that is deliberate, you planned or decided to do it beforehand, and so it happens on purpose rather than by chance.

dense (denser, densest) ADJ
If a text is dense, it contains a lot of information and is difficult to understand.

dispute (disputes) N-VAR
A dispute is an argument or disagreement between people or groups.

disseminate (disseminates, disseminating, disseminated) VERB
To disseminate information or knowledge means to distribute it so that it reaches many people or organizations.

distinguish (distinguishes, distinguishing, distinguished) VERB
If you can distinguish one thing from another or distinguish between two things, you can see or understand how they are different.

distort (distorts, distorting, distorted) VERB
If you distort a statement, fact, or idea, you report or represent it in an untrue way.

e

editor (editors) N-COUNT
An editor is a person who collects pieces of writing by different authors and prepares them for publication in a book or series of books.

et al. ABBREVIATION
et al. is used after a name or a list of names to indicate that other people are also involved. It is used especially when referring to books or articles which were written by more than two people.

evaluate (evaluates, evaluating, evaluated) VERB
If you evaluate something or someone, you consider them in order to make a judgement about them, for example about how good or bad they are.

executive summary (executive summaries) N-COUNT
An executive summary is a summary of a report, generally longer and more detailed than an abstract, which may be read in place of the full report.

expertise N-UNCOUNT
Expertise is special skill or knowledge that is acquired by training, study, or practice.

f

frame (frames, framing, framed) VERB
When you frame information or a question, you arrange, express, or present it in a particular way for a particular purpose.

framework (frameworks) N-COUNT
A framework is a particular set of ideas, rules, or beliefs which you use in order to complete a task or deal with a situation.

fraud (frauds) N-VAR
Fraud is the crime of gaining money or financial benefits by a trick or by lying.

g

gregarious ADJ
Someone who is gregarious enjoys being with other people.

h

heading (headings) N-COUNT
A heading is the title of a piece of writing, which is written or printed at the top.

hierarchical ADJ
A hierarchical system or organization is one in which people have different ranks or positions, depending on how important they are.

humanities N-PLURAL
The humanities are the subjects such as history, languages, literature, and philosophy, which are concerned with human ideas and behaviour.

hypothesis (hypotheses) N-VAR
A hypothesis is an idea which is suggested as a possible explanation for a particular situation or condition, but has not yet been proved to be correct.

i

impact (impacts) N-COUNT
The impact that something has on a situation, process, or person is a sudden and powerful effect that it has on them.

incorporate (incorporates, incorporating, incorporated) VERB
If someone or something is incorporated into a large group, system, or area, they become part of it.

in-depth ADJ
An in-depth study is done in a very careful, thorough, and detailed way.

index (indexes) N-COUNT
An index is an alphabetical list that is printed at the back of a book and tells you on which pages important topics are referred to.

inevitable ADJ
If something is inevitable, it is certain to happen and cannot be prevented or avoided.

infer (infers, inferring, inferred) VERB
If you infer that something is the case, you decide that it is true on the basis of information that you already have.

innate ADJ
An innate quality or ability is one which a person is born with.

intellectual property N-UNCOUNT
Intellectual property is an idea, design, or invention that belongs to the person who created it, and that the law will not allow anyone else to copy.

intensive reading N-UNCOUNT
Intensive reading is careful, detailed reading.

intranet (intranets) N-COUNT
An intranet is a network of computers, similar to the internet, within a particular company or organization.

issue (issues) N-COUNT
An issue of something such as a journal, magazine, or newspaper is the version of it that is published, for example, in a particular month or on a particular day.

k

knowledge claim (knowledge claims) N-COUNT
A knowledge claim is a statement of what you believe to be true.

l

line of reasoning (lines of reasoning) N-COUNT [usu sing]
In a text, the line of reasoning is the way in which the author's thoughts and argument develop.

linear ADJ
A linear process or development is one in which something changes or progresses straight from

one stage to another, and has a starting point and an ending point.

linguist (linguists) N-COUNT
A linguist is a person who studies how language works.

loop (loops) N-COUNT
A loop is a process or series in which the end is connected to the beginning.

m

main clause (main clauses) N-COUNT
The main clause in a complex sentence is the group of words that contains at least a subject and a verb, and can stand alone as a complete sentence.

mind map (mind maps) N-COUNT
A mind map is a diagram used to represent ideas that are linked to and arranged around a central idea.

misconception (misconceptions) N-COUNT
A misconception is an idea that is not correct.

monograph (monographs) N-COUNT
A monograph is a book which is a detailed study of only one subject.

n

notable ADJ
Someone or something that is notable is important or interesting.

notion (notions) N-COUNT
A notion is an idea or belief about something.

noun phrase (noun phrases) N-COUNT
A noun phrase is a noun or pronoun, or a group of words based on a noun or pronoun.

o

objective ADJ
If someone is objective, they base their opinions on facts rather than on their personal feelings.

obstacle (obstacles) N-COUNT
An obstacle is anything that makes it difficult for you to do something.

omit (omits, omitting, omitted) VERB
If you omit something, you do not include it in an activity or piece of work, deliberately or accidentally.

op. cit. ABBREVIATION
op. cit. is used after an author's name to refer to a work of theirs which has already been mentioned.

overview (overviews) N-COUNT
An overview of a situation is a general understanding or description of it as a whole.

overwhelming ADJ
If something is overwhelming, it affects you very strongly, and you do not know how to deal with it.

p

padding N-UNCOUNT
Padding is unnecessary words or information used to make a piece of writing or a speech longer.

paraphrase (paraphrases) N-COUNT
A paraphrase of something written or spoken is the same thing expressed in a different way.

PDF (PDFs) N-COUNT
PDF files are computer documents which look exactly like the original documents, regardless of which software or operating system was used to create them.

peer reviewed ADJ
An academic text or piece of work which is peer reviewed has been judged by other academic experts working in the same area.

perceive (perceives, perceiving, perceived) VERB
If you perceive someone or something as doing or being a particular thing, it is your opinion that they do this thing or that they are that thing.

perfectionist (perfectionists) N-COUNT
Someone who is a perfectionist refuses to do or accept anything that is not as good as it could possibly be.

perspective (perspectives) N-COUNT
A particular perspective is a particular way of thinking about something, especially one that is influenced by your beliefs or experiences.

persuasive ADJ
Someone who is persuasive is likely to persuade a person to believe or do a particular thing.

plagiarize (plagiarizes, plagiarizing, plagiarized) VERB
If someone plagiarizes another person's idea or work, they use it or copy it and pretend that they thought of it or created it.

pose (poses, posing, posed) VERB
If you pose a question, you ask a question, especially one that needs serious consideration. If something poses a challenge or a problem, it is the cause of that challenge or problem that has to be dealt with.

position (positions) N-COUNT
Your position on a particular matter is your attitude towards it or your opinion of it.

preamble (preambles) N-VAR
A preamble is an introduction that comes before something you say or write.

prefix (prefixes) N-COUNT
A prefix is a letter or a group of letters, for example 'un-' or 'multi-', which is added to the beginning of a word in order to form a different word.

premise (premises) N-COUNT
A premise is something that you suppose is true and that you use as a basis for developing an idea

prescribed ADJ
A prescribed book or text is one that has to be read for a particular course.

principal ADJ
Principal means first in order of importance.

prominent ADJ
Something that is prominent is very noticeable or is an important part of something else.

proofread (proofreads, proofreading, proofread) VERB
When someone proofreads something such as a book or an article, they read it before it is published or submitted in order to find and mark mistakes that need to be corrected.

r

rationale (rationales) N-COUNT
The rationale for a course of action, practice, or belief is the set of reasons on which it is based.

recall (recalls, recalling, recalled) VERB
If a library recalls a book, it asks the person who has borrowed it to return it.

receptive ADJ
Someone who is receptive to new ideas or suggestions is prepared to consider them or accept them.

reflect on (reflects on, reflecting on, reflected on) VERB
When you reflect on something, you think deeply about it.

regression (regressions) N-VAR
Regression is the act of returning to an earlier and less advanced stage of development.

reliable ADJ
People or things that are reliable can be trusted to work well or to behave in the way that you want them to.

renew (renews, renewing, renewed) VERB
If you renew a book from a library, you borrow it for a further period of time.

replicate (replicates, replicating, replicated) VERB
If you replicate someone's experiment, work, or research, you do it yourself in exactly the same way.

repository (repositories) N-COUNT
A repository is a place where something is kept safely.

representative ADJ
Someone who is typical of the group to which they belong can be described as representative.

reprint (reprints) N-COUNT
A reprint is a new copy of a book or article, printed because all the other ones have been sold or because minor changes have been made to the original.

reserve (reserves, reserving, reserved) VERB
If something is reserved for a particular person or purpose, it is kept specially for that person or purpose.

retain (retains, retaining, retained) VERB
To retain something means to keep or continue to have that thing.

s

sample (samples) N-COUNT
A sample of people or things is a number of them chosen out of a larger group and then used in tests or used to provide information about the whole group.

scan (scans, scanning, scanned) VERB
When you scan written material, you look through it quickly in order to find important or interesting information.

scepticism N-UNCOUNT
Scepticism is great doubt about whether something is true or useful.

scholar (scholars) N-COUNT
A scholar is a person who studies an academic subject and knows a lot about it.

scope N-SING
The scope of an activity, topic, or piece of work is the whole area which it deals with or includes.

screen (screens, screening, screened) VERB
If you screen something, you check it systematically to decide whether it is suitable.

search engine (search engines) N-COUNT
A search engine is a computer program that searches for documents containing a particular word or words on the internet.

seminal ADJ
A seminal work is an important and influential work.

sentence fragment (sentence fragments) N-COUNT
A sentence fragment is a clause or phrase that is punctuated as a sentence but is not a grammatically complete sentence.

sic ADV
You write sic in brackets after a word or expression when you want to indicate to the reader that although the word looks odd or wrong, you intended to write it like that or the original writer wrote it like that.

signposting expression (signposting expressions) N-COUNT
A signposting expression in a text is a word or phrase that shows how ideas are connected and helps the reader follow the text.

skim (skims, skimming, skimmed) VERB
If you skim a piece of writing, you read through it quickly in order to get a general idea of its content.

source material (source materials) N-VAR
Source materials are books, articles, and other documents that provide information for a piece of research.

statistical ADJ
Statistical evidence is obtained by analysing information expressed as numbers, for example information about the number of times that something happens.

stimulate (stimulates, stimulating, stimulated) VERB
To stimulate something means to encourage it to begin or develop further.

strategy (strategies) N-VAR
A strategy is a general plan intended to achieve something.

subheading (subheadings) N-COUNT
Subheadings are titles that divide part of a piece of writing into shorter sections.

subject discipline (subject disciplines) N-COUNT
In an academic setting, a subject discipline is a particular topic or specific area of study.

subordinate ADJ
Something that is subordinate to something else is less important than the other thing.

subsidiary ADJ
If something is subsidiary, it is less important than something else with which it is connected.

substantial ADJ
Substantial means large in amount or degree.

subtext (subtexts) N-VAR
The subtext is the implied message or subject of something that is said or written.

subvocalize (subvocalizes, subvocalizing, subvocalized) VERB
If you subvocalize when you are reading a text, you move your mouth as if you are speaking the words.

suffix (suffixes) N-COUNT
A suffix is a letter or a group of letters, for example '-ly' or '-ness', which is added to the end of a word in order to form a different word, often of a different word class.

supporting evidence N-UNCOUNT
Supporting evidence is information that is used to prove something.

survey (surveys, surveying, surveyed) VERB
If you survey a text, you look quickly through it to discover its main features.

synonym (synonyms) N-COUNT
A synonym is a word or expression which means the same as another word or expression.

synthesize (synthesizes, synthesizing, synthesized) VERB
If you synthesize different ideas, you combine these ideas.

t

text box (text boxes) N-COUNT
A text box is a rectangular box containing a piece of text.

theoretical framework (theoretical frameworks) N-COUNT
A theoretical framework is a set of ideas used to analyse something or make judgements about it.

theoretical perspective (theoretical perspectives) N-COUNT
If you examine something from a theoretical perspective, you consider the ideas and abstract principles relating to it rather than its practical aspects or uses.

topic sentence (topic sentences) N-COUNT
A topic sentences is a sentence which states the topic or main point of a paragraph.

trait (traits) N-COUNT
A trait is a particular characteristic, quality, or tendency that someone or something has.

truncate (truncates, truncating, truncated) VERB
To truncate something is to shorten it.

u

URL (URLs) N-COUNT
A URL is an address that shows where a particular page can be found on the World Wide Web.

v

validity N-UNCOUNT
The validity of something such as a result or a piece of information is whether it can be trusted or believed.

value N-UNCOUNT
The value of something such as a quality, attitude, or method is its importance or usefulness

(values, valuing, valued) VERB
If you value something or someone, you think that they are important and you appreciate them.
N-PLURAL The values of a person or group are the moral principles and beliefs that they think are important.

verifiable ADJ
Something that is verifiable can be proved to be true or genuine.

vested interest (vested interests) N-VAR
If you have a vested interest in something, you have a strong reason for acting in a particular way, for example to protect your money, power, or reputation.

visceral ADJ
Visceral feelings are feelings that you feel very deeply and find it difficult to control or ignore, and that are not the result of thought.

volume (volumes) N-COUNT
A volume is a collection of several issues of a journal, for example all the issues for one year.

w

whitelisting N-UNCOUNT
Whitelisting is the creation of a list of people who a person or organization considers to be safe and trustworthy, and who they are happy to allow onto their computer networks, or from whom they are happy to receive electronic data and e-mails.

Answer key

Chapter 1

Exercise 1
Read the responses and comments from two successful university students below:

Naoko, first year economics student

Stage	Tasks	√	Time
1 Preparation	Think about the research topic and the instructions given.	√	1 day
	Find out what information is available – do some background reading.		
	Devise a rough outline plan.	√	1/2 day
2 Gathering information	Gather books and articles from the library or online.	√	1 day
	Read and take notes.	√	6–7 days
3 Writing up	Write a more detailed plan.		
	Write a first draft.	√	9–10 days
	Revise your first draft.	√	2 days
	Write a second draft.	√	9–10 days
	Proofread your second draft and make corrections.	√	1 day

'I have written two research assignments so far. We can choose which questions to answer from a list, so I choose ones that are clear and easy for me to answer. Also, we are at the beginning of our course, so the lecturers give us a lot of information about the sources we can use. So, in a way I have already done background reading as part of my course. I'm quite a slow writer, so when I have an assignment I spend most of my time writing. I like to work out my ideas by writing.'

Illaria, third year literature student

Stage	Tasks	√	Time
1 Preparation	Think about the research topic and the instructions given.	√	3 days
	Find out what information is available – do some background reading.	√	1–2 days
	Devise a rough outline plan.	√	1/2 day
2 Gathering information	Gather books and articles from the library or online.	√	1 day
	Read and take notes.	√	12–14 days
3 Writing up	Write a more detailed plan.	√	1–2 days
	Write a first draft.	√	4–5 days
	Revise your first draft.	√	2 days
	Write a second draft.	√	3–4 days
	Proofread your second draft and make corrections.	√	1 day

'I'm used to writing research assignments now – but they are still difficult! I need to spend a lot of time thinking before I can write something down. I usually need at least two weeks to find interesting sources and read. That's very important for my course. If I do those things well, the writing usually goes quite quickly. If I can, I try to take a break for one or two days before writing the second draft. I think it's important to give yourself a break from your research sometimes.'

Exercise 2
a If you do this, you will not show all of the skills that you need to demonstrate. In particular you will not show that you have good critical thinking skills. To make your argument strong, you need to show that you have considered other points of view and to explain why you do not agree with them.

b This is the best approach. It would allow you to demonstrate all of the skills required to achieve a good mark. Showing that you have considered the question from more than one point of view will make your essay more convincing to the reader.

c This is not a good approach. You may show that you can work hard at certain skills, but you will not be able to demonstrate the really important critical thinking skills: evaluating the work of other scholars and synthesizing the information and ideas into a convincing argument.

Exercise 3

1 discuss, examines

2 outlines, assess

3 trace, compare and contrast

4 justify

Exercise 4

1 f 2 c 3 g 4 e 5 a 6 d 7 h 8 b

Exercise 5

1 **Comment on** – give your *informed* opinion about something (Note: your opinion should be informed by your study of the topic)

2 **Illustrate** – give examples and evidence to show how something works or that something is true

3 **Relate** – show the connections between two things

Exercise 6

Suggested answers:

1 b compare, c contrast, f give an account, h outline, i trace

2 a assess, d discuss, e examine, g justify, j comment on, k illustrate, l relate

3 discuss

Exercise 7

Suggested answers:

1 Types of films could include: action, anime, children's, comedy, documentary, horror, independent, low budget, short.

2 You could define 'successful' as: winning awards, attracting a large audience, or being highly rated by film critics.

Chapter 2

Self-evaluation

All four sources of information may be useful. Course reading lists and handouts are often a good place to start. Your university library and academic databases can provide good quality, 'peer reviewed' source texts. Google™ is easy to access, but it is advisable to use Google Scholar™ for academic material.

Exercise 1

1 c 2 a 3 b 4 d

Exercise 2

	Type of publication	Search terms
1	book	Small, G., & Vorgan, G.; *iBrain: surviving the technological alteration of the modern mind*
2	journal article	Semanza, J. C.; *American Journal of Public Health*
3	journal article	Inceoglu, I., Segers, J., & Bartram, D.; *Journal of Occupational & Organizational Psychology*
4	book	Chan, K. W., Kwong, C. K., & Dillon, T. S.; *Computational intelligence techniques for new product design*

Exercise 3

Suggested answers:

1 Assess the European Central Bank's response to the Eurozone financial crisis.

2 Compare and contrast social media use among young people in the United States and in China.

3 Give an account of the role of ribonucleic acid in protein synthesis.

4 Trace the history of the comic book.

Exercise 5
Suggested answers:

1 banking crisis/credit crunch

2 online social networking/e-network

3 youth/young adults

4 graphic novel

Exercise 6
For a general idea of what you can expect, see answers to questions 1–5 below based on the University of Glasgow library.

1 Up to 30 items in total from the main collection (10 items maximum from short loan).

2 4 weeks for most items (between 4 hours and 1 week for short loan items).

3 Yes, you can reserve and renew items online – however, if you owe money for an item that is overdue, you must pay the fine and renew the item in person.

4 Yes, 5 pence per day for most items, 50 pence per hour for short loan items.

5 Log onto your library account and use the 'Article Reach' facility.

Exercise 7
1 "media coverage", "2008 banking crisis"

2 "life partner", "Abraham Maslow", "hierarchy of needs"

3 "electricity generation", "wind power", "environmental impact"

4 "online social networking"

Exercise 8
Suggested answers:

1 environment* – environments, environmentalist, environmentally

2 network* – networks, networked

3 friend* – friend, friends, friendly, friendliness

Exercise 9
Suggested answers:

1 Is <u>generosity</u> an <u>innate</u> <u>human</u> <u>trait</u>?

2 altruism (= unselfish concern for other people's happiness and welfare)

3 "innate human trait"

4 generosity *or* altruism *and* "innate human trait"

Exercise 10
Google ™ will generate some scholarly items but it will also show items from commercial sites, newspapers, online encyclopaedias and so on. Google Scholar™ will generate scholarly items.

Chapter 3

Exercise 1
1 d 2 e 3 a 4 f 5 c 6 b

Exercise 2
Although the author writes for popular media, she does have academic credentials. She holds a PhD from a respected university and is a visiting lecturer at another well-known university. She is also a member of two widely recognized scientific associations and an associate editor of an academic journal.

Exercise 3
1 The .com suffix indicates this is a commercial publication. *Scientific American* is a good quality magazine. However, as it is not written specifically for an academic audience, you should verify with your lecturers that it is alright to use this source.

2 The .co.uk suffix indicates that this is a commercial news site. It is widely respected but not generally considered suitable for academic citation.

3 This is an online encyclopaedia. The information is not 'peer-reviewed', so it is not considered suitable for academic citation.

4 The .edu suffix indicates that this is an educational site, so the material is likely to be academically credible.

5 This is a commercial site which sells essays online. Information from this type of site should not be cited in an essay.

Exercise 4
No, it has not been written for an academic audience because it is too informal in style. Although it mentions the names of scientists, the style and the use of contractions such as 'don't' show the informality of the article. It is possibly an article in a newspaper or magazine.

Exercise 5
1 we

2 He uses their full names: Felix Warneken and Michel Tomasello

3 the dash

4 We've, don't

5 *chimpanzee* has been abbreviated to *chimp*

6 something, science

7 fascinating; give … a hand

8 all

Exercise 6
1 Although the title looks potentially relevant (e.g. 'cures'), the date (2000) indicates the item is too old.

2 The title doesn't specifically mention the 2008 crisis but the word 'aftermath' suggests it may be relevant.

3 Probably not relevant as the focus is on causes.

4 Appears to be relevant.

5 Probably not relevant as the focus is on developing countries not on the European Union.

Exercise 7
The abstract describes a study of the impact of Facebook use on undergraduate students, and would therefore not be directly relevant to young people between the ages of 12 and 16. However, the study could be useful for background information and as a point of comparison.

Chapter 4

Exercise 1
There are:

statement of aims at the start of each chapter

headings and subheadings

bulleted lists

text boxes

glossary of key words

review section at the end of each chapter

Exercise 2

Model answer:

This answer is based on Chapter 1 of EAP Research Skills.

1 I noticed all five features a-e.

2 The headings, lists and diagrams were the most useful. I noticed the heading 'How do you know if your research is good?' and the list of marking criteria under it because that is something that I'm concerned about. I also noticed the diagrams showing the parts of an essay question. Giving the information this way made it easier to understand. The list at the end was also useful; it gave me an idea of which parts of the chapter I wanted to study in more detail.

3 I tried reading Chapter 2 from start to finish without surveying it first. When I compare that experience with the method I used to read Chapter 1, I think that I felt more motivated to read Chapter 1. It was easier to focus on the information I was most interested it. When I read Chapter 2, I noticed that I sometimes lost concentration because I wasn't always sure about why I was reading the information – I just read it because it was there.

Exercise 4
1 discussion – in this section the authors explain their findings ('We argue that this effect may be the result of …') and assess their significance ('Our study provides evidence of Facebook's unique contributions to …').

2 introduction – in this this section the authors present the context of the research ('Facebook is a rapidly expanding phenomenon … Anecdotal evidence … suggests …') and explain why the research was done ('The objectives of the present study were …').

3 methods – in this section the authors describe how the research was done ('Three hundred eight undergraduate students completed an online survey …').

4 results – in this section the authors present their findings ('A hierarchical multiple regression analysis … revealed …').

The original order was: 2, 3, 4, 1

Exercise 5

1 The author is exploring the theme of leadership crisis and leadership emergence in four animated films.

2 The author uses two theoretical approaches: psychoanalysis and structuralist film studies.

3 The films represent leadership crisis and emergence as myths in which the young defeat evil power figures through a process of self-discovery and maturation. The study can give the reader insights into popular views of leadership and the relationship between leadership and social organizations.

Exercise 6

Section 2: 'The funding crisis to date' most clearly discusses a problem.

Section 4: 'The architecture of reform' and Section 5: 'Future funding of care' discuss solutions.

Chapter 5

Exercise 1

1 The first sentence

2 'In a famous study …'

Exercise 2

1 Yes, it is relevant because it discusses a theory of why people form relationships.

2 Yes, they state that the theory 'has a future' and that it is often used.

3 You could use the words: 'goods, information, love, money, services and status' from the fourth paragraph.

4 You would read the sixth paragraph which begins with the topic sentence: 'A final important concept in social exchange theory is the part played by each person's comparison level or CL – a standard against which all of one's relationships are judged.'

Exercise 3

1 Clore

2 1961

3 rewarding – it makes one feel good

4 the section before the extract – proximity is mentioned in the first paragraph

Exercise 5

1 b   2 b   3 b   4 a   5 b   6 a

Exercise 6

The Wikipedia entry may be useful because it:

- gives several synonyms for 'attribution error' ('attribution effect' and 'actor-observer bias')

- uses different wording to define the concept and highlights the key words ('the tendency to over-value dispositional or personality-based explanations for the observed behaviors of others while under-valuing situational explanations for those behaviors.')

- provides a simple example ('consider a situation where a driver, Alice, is about to pass through an intersection …')

Chapter 6

Exercise 2

Possible questions might include:

1 In what way is Facebook changing the nature of social relationships?

2 How does Facebook create jealousy?

3 How did the researchers explore the role of Facebook in creating jealousy?

4 What is a 'hierarchical multiple regression analysis?'

5 Why does increased use of Facebook make people more likely to experience Facebook-related jealousy?

6 Is Facebook the only cause of jealousy in romantic relationships?

Exercise 4

1 adverb, contrasting term (for 'unconcerned'). If you do something **eagerly**, you do it in a way that shows you want to do it or have something very much.

2 noun, general term. A **trait** is a particular characteristic or quality.

3 noun, cause (of loyalty). If someone has **charisma**, they can attract, influence, and inspire people.

4 adjective, synonym (for 'secretive' in the following sentence). Something that is **clandestine** is kept secret, often because it is bad or illegal.

5 noun, result (of experiencing 'frequent criticism in childhood'). **Inhibition** is a feeling of fear or embarrassment that makes it difficult for you to behave naturally.

Exercise 5

1 both   2 before   3 true   4 over   5 make

Exercise 6

1 anti = against, opposed; wise = way or in relation to; anticlockwise = (adverb and adjective) moving in the opposite direction in which the hands of a clock move

2 dis = opposite of; close = shut; disclosure = (noun) the act of giving people new or secret information

3 un = opposite of; fore = before; seen = past participle of see; unforeseen = (adjective) not expected to happen or known about beforehand

4 mono = one; theos = god; ism = noun referring to political or religious movements and beliefs; monotheism = (noun) belief in one god

5 de = removal of; ation = process; deforestation = (noun) the process of removing or destroying forests

6 uni = one; form = shape; uniformity = (noun) a state or condition in which everything is regular or the same

7 semi = partly; detached = past participle of detach = separate; semi-detached = (adjective) partly separated (used to describe a house which is joined to another house by one shared wall)

8 bi = two; lingu = language; bilingual = (adjective) involving or using two languages

9 contra = against; dict = speak; contradict = (verb) to deny the truth of a statement by saying the opposite

10 pre = before; precondition = (noun) a condition that must be fulfilled before something else can happen

Exercise 9

> **Model answer:**
>
> For many, | the need for knowledge | about their partner's intent | becomes indispensable, | and several participants | specifically mentioned | the word "addiction" | in relation | to their own Facebook usage.

Chapter 7

Exercise 1

All of these statements are presented as facts but actually express opinions.

1 The term 'too expensive' is imprecise and subjective.

2 expresses a value judgement

3 makes a prediction

4 expresses a cause and effect relationship regarding a complex phenomenon which would be difficult to verify experimentally

5 makes a categorical assertion

6 expresses a cause and effect relationship regarding a complex phenomenon that would not be possible to verify experimentally

7 'women' implies all women and is therefore categorical; 'always' is also a categorical term; 'ambitious' is an imprecise term

8 'immoral' is an imprecise term and expresses a value judgement

9 expresses a value judgement; the superlative 'finest' is a categorical term

10 makes a prediction; 'never' is a categorical term

Exercise 4

1 The extract describes the research area as consisting of two main viewpoints: one based on evolutionary theory and the other on social learning theory, plus a third 'biosocial' perspective.

2 All of these perspectives would ideally be explored further.

Exercise 5

1 The experimenters appear to be working within a social learning perspective, that is with the belief that human behaviour is generally learned rather than biologically determined. They would therefore argue that generosity is not innate.

2 People learn to act generously by imitating models.

3 In an experiment, they observed that motorists were significantly more likely to assist a woman stranded at the side of the road if they had recently observed someone else doing so.

4 The motorists who stopped did so because they wanted to be helpful.

Exercise 6

assumptions ⟶ The social network site Facebook is a rapidly expanding phenomenon that is changing the nature of social relationships. […]The objectives of the present study were to explore the role of Facebook in the experience of jealousy and to determine if increased Facebook exposure

predicts jealousy above and beyond personal and relationship factors. Three hundred eight undergraduate students completed an online survey that assessed demographic and personality factors and explored respondents' Facebook use. A hierarchical multiple regression analysis, controlling for individual, personality, and relationship factors, revealed that increased Facebook use significantly predicts Facebook-related jealousy. ⟵ evidence

We argue that this effect may be the result of a feedback loop whereby using Facebook exposes people to often ambiguous information about their partner that they may not otherwise have access to and that this new information incites further Facebook use. ⟵ reasoning

Our study provides evidence of Facebook's unique contributions to the experience of jealousy in romantic relationships. ⟵ position

Chapter 8

Exercise 2

Cross out f.

Introduction

c, k

1 Traits approach

   a, j, i, d, g, l   (OR: j, a, i, d, g, l)

2 Situational theories

   e, b, h   (OR: b, e, h)

Exercise 3

1 The student has misspelled 'Ringelmann' and copied text word-for-word without using quotation marks.

2 The student has put copied text in quotation marks but changed the wording ('although' at the start of the sentence has been substituted with 'but'); also the page number hasn't been noted.

3 The information is incorrect.

Exercise 4

Model answer:

1 There are 3 main types of company

   a sole trader – most common type of company

   b partnership – 2nd most common

   c corporation – different from sole trader & partnership; 'separate legal entity'

2 Different leadership skills needed for different types of enterprises

   a Corporations require leaders able to manage large teams & operate strategically

Exercise 5

main features	**2** Situational theories
	a Emphasis of situational theories: situation is important; no single style of leadership suitable for all situations
	b Tannenbaum & Schmidt (1973) one of 1st to devise situational model
example study	**c** According to Tannenbaum & Schmidt (1973), some situations require 'boss-centred' leadership, others require 'subordinate-centred leadership

Exercise 6

Approach	Main features	Examples	Strengths	Problems
Traits	*1 a*	1 c	1 b	1 d, 1 e & 1f
Situational	2 a	2 b & 2 c	____	____

Exercise 7

Extract 1

Relationships progress when:

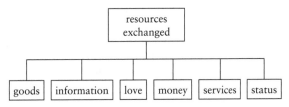

Foa and Foa (1975) in Hogg & Vaughan (2011)

Extract 2

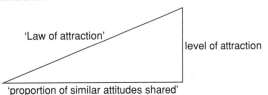

Clore (1976) in Hogg & Vaughan (2011)

Extract 3

Facebook use & jealousy

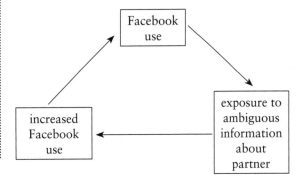

Muise, Christofides & Desmarais, S. (2009)

Exercise 8

Wheel or Star network

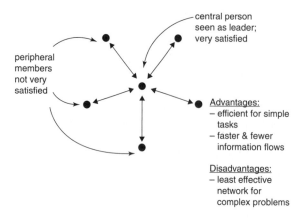

central person
seen as leader;
very satisfied

peripheral
members
not very
satisfied

Advantages:
– efficient for simple
  tasks
– faster & fewer
  information flows

Disadvantages:
– least effective
  network for
  complex problems

Exercise 10

Situational theories

1 Limitations

a right knowledge & abilities sometimes ≠ leadership

b impact differences in interpersonal & leadership style not explained

c not always feasible for situation → choice of leader

2 Strengths

a situational factors still considered significant

b situational variables + leadership behaviour = contingency theory

Points 2 a and 2 b, which describe strengths, can be put in the first empty box in Exercise 6; points 1a, 1 b and 1 c, which describe problems, can be put in the second empty box.

Chapter 9

Exercise 1

In the introduction she included b and f because she wanted to contextualize and defend her choice of topic at the very start of her essay.

In the conclusion she included e because she wanted remind the reader of her most important points and encourage the reader to look to the future.

In the body she covered subtopics a, d and finally c because she wanted to begin with features that are relatively obvious and straightforward to describe and finish with features that are less obvious and require more analysis.

Exercise 2

e – motivates the reader by explaining why the topic is important

a and c – contextualize the essay by describing the research area

b – states the purpose (= 'aim') of the essay

d – describes the plan

Exercise 3

Model answers:

Block format:

1 Similarities between Twitter and Weibo:

a rapidly expanding, large numbers of users

b can post messages up to 140 characters, pictures & video

c increase flow of information

d mainly used for socializing

d loss making

e government censorship

2 Differences between Twitter and Weibo:

a Twitter came first (2006 vs 2009 for Weibo)

b Twitter is global and multilingual; Weibo in China & Mandarin only

c Weibo often used for product information

d Weibo 1st to introduce picture & video

e Twitter losing more money ($26m vs $14m for Weibo)

f Twitter advocates free speech; Weibo advocates self-censorship

f complete government control of Weibo; Twitter censored in some countries but not others

Feature-by-feature format:

1 History

  a similarity: both recent

  b difference: Twitter came first (2006 vs 2009 for Weibo); but Weibo 1ˢᵗ to introduce picture & video

2 Demographic

  a similarity: rapidly expanding, large numbers of users

  b difference: Twitter global & multilingual; Weibo in China & Mandarin only

3 Services

  a similarity: users can post messages up to 140 characters, pictures & video

  b difference: –

4 Use

  a similarity: increase flow of information; socializing

  b difference: Weibo often used for product information

5 Profitability

  a similarity: loss making

  b differences: Twitter losing more money ($26m vs $14m for Weibo)

6 Government control

  a similarity: government control

  b difference: Twitter advocates free speech; Weibo self-censorship; complete government control of Weibo; Twitter censored in some countries but not others

Feature-by-feature format generally allows for more detailed comparison.

Exercise 4

1 unhelpful – if you do not consider your opponent's point of view they are unlikely to remain in the discussion

2 unhelpful – if your opponent has no reason to believe there is anything wrong with their own point of view, they are unlikely to consider an alternative point of view

3 helpful – your opponent is more likely to engage in the discussion if they feel you respect their way of thinking

4 unhelpful – your opponent is unlikely to accept criticism from you if you are unwilling to think critically about your own point of view

5 helpful – your opponent is more likely to accept your point of view if they can see how it relates to their own way of thinking

6 helpful – your opponent is unlikely to accept what you say simply because you say it

7 helpful – your opponent is more likely to listen if they feel heard, but making the final point is advantageous because it often has more impact than points scored earlier in the argument

Exercise 5

1 Points a and b follow the general to specific format. It is useful to discuss the support for the viewpoint (c) before moving on to the problems (d) because you can then introduce the next point of view as a response to those problems.

2 The last problem with the Traits approach mentioned in part 1d is that the Traits approach does not adequately account for the fact that not all leaders are equally effective in different situations. This provides a logical 'bridge' to the next viewpoint considered: the Situational approach, which argues precisely that the situation must be taken into consideration when discussing leadership.

3 Academic arguments generally proceed step-by-step towards the conclusion with 'stronger' points of view presented after 'weaker' points of view have been dismissed. Therefore, the writer can be assumed to favour the Situational approach.

Exercise 7

According to the guideline: 1 e, 2 c, 3 a, 4 d, 5 b

However, other sequences are possible, for example, e (the rationale) could be placed in the middle after a (description of approaches) or at the very end.

Exercise 8

Model answer:

Introduction

 a Rationale: why pupil performance in language, maths & science is worth studying

 b Context: what is happening in education generally

 c Purpose: explain changes in performance

 d Plan: 1st compare & contrast 2007 & 2012 figures; consider educational policy as a factor; examine other factor(s)

Body

1 Comparison 2007 & 2012 figures

 a similarities: what hasn't changed?

 b differences: what has changed?

2 Changes due to educational policy

 a general description of changes in education policy

 b specific examples

 c support for this factor as a cause of changes in pupil performance

 d problems with this explanation

3 Changes due to another factor

 a general description of this factor

 b specific examples

 c support for this view

 d problems with this view

Conclusion

 a Rationale: why the topic is important

 b Summary: 2007 & 2012 pupil performance were compared, factors that may explain changes in pupil performance were discussed

 c Opinion: factor discussed in section 3 more important (or both factors important)

 d Suggestions for future action: what can be done to improve pupil performance

 e Suggestions for future research: what needs to be investigated further for a better understanding of this issue

Chapter 10

Self-evaluation

All of the statements are false.

1 Essays at undergraduate and Master's degree level are not expected to contain original ideas. Your originality is in the way you combine source material and present your argument.

2 It is usually much more common to paraphrase or summarize source material than to quote it word-for-word. In most cases, you should only quote word-for-word if the language of the original text is special in some way.

3 To paraphrase a text, you should substantially reword it.

4 All source materials must be referenced, whether you summarize, paraphrase or quote them word-for word.

5 You must reference source materials, whatever your opinion is about them.

Exercise 1

1 c 2 a 3 g 4 e 5 b 6 d 7 f

Exercise 2

1 There are 3 sources used: IC3, UKCA, Smith *et al.* The first and second source texts provide evidence to support the writers claim; the third source supports the writer's view with expert opinion.

2 The first two sources are paraphrased, the third is quoted word-for-word.

3 The first two are paraphrased because it is the information, not the language, that is important; the third expresses a somewhat controversial point and uses colourful language.

Exercise 3

1 provide evidence to support the claim – paraphrase

2 no source material needed

3 provide evidence to support the claim – paraphrase

4 provide evidence to support the claim – paraphrase, OR support the view with expert opinion – possibly a quote from someone with inside knowledge of banks

5 provide evidence to support the claim – paraphrase, OR support the view with expert opinion – possibly a quote from someone with inside knowledge of banks

6 support the view with expert opinion – probably a quote because the statement is controversial

Exercise 4

In sentence 1, the word 'psychological' has been italicized, but the writer has not indicated that this is his emphasis.

In sentence 2, the writer has replaced the word 'victims' with the pronoun 'they' and omitted to use quotation marks around the word 'stupid'.

In sentence 3, the word 'we' has been omitted but not replaced with […].

Finally, no page number has been given in the reference.

The essay extract should read:

The impact of fraud on victims can be significant. According to the UK Office of Fair Trading (2009: 8), 'Scams cause *psychological* as well as financial harm to victims (my emphasis). Victims not only suffer a financial loss, but also a loss of self-esteem because they blame themselves for having been so 'stupid' to fall for the scam. Some of the victims […] interviewed appeared to have been seriously damaged by their experience'.

Exercise 5

> **Model answer:**
>
> According to the UK Office of Fair Trading (2009: 8), people who fall prey to fraudsters are not only robbed of their money but also experience psychological harm. They may feel ashamed for having been gullible, and consequently, lose self-confidence. For some, the effects seem to be very harmful.

Exercise 6

In sentence 1, the writer has used too much of the original vocabulary; the grammar has been changed but results in an awkward 'jumbled' sentence.

Sentence 2 is acceptable; it retains the meaning of the source text but is substantially different in terms of vocabulary and grammar.

Sentence 3 retains too much of the original sentence structure and vocabulary (only two words have been changed: 'victims' and 'appeared'). Also, the pronoun 'we' now appears to refer to the student writer rather than the authors of the source material.

Exercise 7

According to the UK Office of Fair Trading (2009: 6), scammers employ two main strategies to encourage people to respond. Firstly, they represent themselves as trustworthy businesses or organisations. Secondly, they appeal to people's emotions in order to discourage them from thinking too carefully about what is being offered. Scammers also reduce victims' ability to think rationally. They hint that because the offer is 'scarce', urgent action is needed. They induce an sense of obligation by making small initial demands. Finally, they reduce the apparent size of the victim's payment by contrasting it to the huge reward on offer.

Chapter 11

Exercise 1

The in-text citations are almost identical. The only difference is that the APA style uses the symbol '&' whereas the *Chicago Manual of Style* uses 'and'.

Research

Exercise 2

It is an article from an online journal.

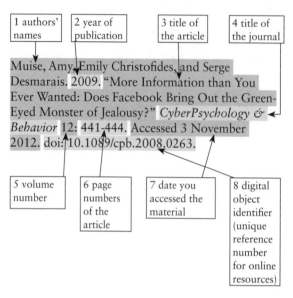

| 1 authors' names | 2 year of publication | 3 title of the article | 4 title of the journal |

Muise, Amy, Emily Christofides, and Serge Desmarais. 2009. "More Information than You Ever Wanted: Does Facebook Bring Out the Green-Eyed Monster of Jealousy?" *CyberPsychology & Behavior* 12: 441–444. Accessed 3 November 2012. doi:10.1089/cpb.2008.0263.

| 5 volume number | 6 page numbers of the article | 7 date you accessed the material | 8 digital object identifier (unique reference number for online resources) |

Exercise 3

1 Example of a chapter in an edited book:

Kelly, John D. 2010. "Seeing Red: Mao Fetishism, Pax Americana, and the Moral Economy of War". In *Anthropology and Global Counterinsurgency*, edited by John D. Kelly, Beatrice Jauregui, Sean T. Mitchell, and Jeremy Walton, 67–83. Chicago: University of Chicago Press.

2 Example of an e-book:

Austen, Jane. 2007. *Pride and Prejudice*. New York: Penguin Classics. Kindle edition.

Kurland, Philip B., and Ralph Lerner, eds. 1987. The Founders' Constitution. Chicago: University of Chicago Press. http://press-pubs.uchicago.edu/founders/.

3 Example of a book review (online):

Kamp, David. 2006. "Deconstructing Dinner." Review of The Omnivore's Dilemma: A Natural History of Four Meals, by Michael Pollan. New York Times, April 23, Sunday Book Review. http://www.nytimes.com/2006/04/23/books/review/23kamp.html.

4 Example of a newspaper:

Mendelsohn, Daniel. 2010. "But Enough about Me." New Yorker, January 25.

Exercise 4

1 Clore, G. L. and D. Byrne. 1974. "A Reinforcement-affect Model of Attraction." In *Foundations of Interpersonal Attraction*, edited by T. L. Huston, 143-165. New York: Academic Press.

2 Rusbult, C. E., J. M. Martz and C. R. Agnew. 1998. "The Investment Model Scale: Measuring Commitment Level, Satisfaction Level, Quality of Alternatives, and Investment Size." *Personal Relationships* 5: 357-391.

3 Smahel, David, Bradford B. Brown, and Lucas Blinka. 2012. "Association between online friendship and Internet addiction among adolescents and emerging adults." *Developmental Psychology* 48: 381-388. Accessed March 3, 2013. doi 10.1037/a0027025.

Exercise 5

In the bibliography the first author's surname precedes the given name, and full stops are used instead of commas. For the book entry, there are no round brackets around the place of publication, publisher, and year of publication.

Exercise 6

Sentences 1, 2 and 4 can be considered general knowledge. Sentences 3 and 5 appear to be the intellectual property of the source text author or authors because they contain information that would need to be gathered by research. Sentences 3 and 5 should therefore be referenced. Remember, if in doubt, give the reference.

Chapter 12

Exercise 1

1 This form of paraphrasing is commonly referred to as 'patchwriting' and is considered by many to be a form of plagiarism.

2 Failure to give in-text citations is a form of plagiarism.

3 Omitting to use quotation marks around directly quoted material is a form of plagiarism.

4 Drawing all of your source material from one or two source texts is not technically plagiarism as long as you cite the material correctly. However,

if you do this your work will not be judged to be sufficiently original. In a research essay, you are expected to synthesize, that is bring together, a variety of source materials.

5 Unless you have been told to collaborate with another student, using work written by another student in your essay is a form of plagiarism.

Exercise 2
The sentence: 'Although a limited form of contact, mobile e-mail has fulfilled a function akin to co-presence for people that lack the means to share the same private physical space (Ito, 2005: 16)' has been copied from the source text word-for-word so should be in quotation marks.

Exercise 3
1 It was necessary to investigate further.

2 It is preferable to have a shorter working week and fewer redundancies even if that means lower take-home pay.

3 It is likely that, within the next five years, schoolchildren will be using mobile devices to learn basic skills in the classroom.

4 There is insufficient evidence of a clear link between online gaming and hyperactivity.

Exercise 4
1 In paragraph 1 the source material is used to provide a classification of cybercrime. In paragraph 2 the source material is used to support the writer's point about the growth in cybercrime.

2 The writer is more in control in paragraph 2 because he is using the source material to support his point not just repeating someone else's point. He also synthesizes several extracts, which indicates greater control. In paragraph 1 the writer's 'voice' is missing because he does not give his opinion of the source material.

3 In the first sentence the writer states his opinion directly by making a claim about cybercrime and in the following sentences supporting that claim with references to data. In the final sentence the writer implies that, like Smith *et al.*, he believes

the internet has become a "playground for criminals" by stating that the evidence supports that claim.

Exercise 5
1 'Suggest' makes the claim less definite or certain.

2 'Assume' means the authors accept that the claim is true without having evidence for it.

3 'Imply' means the authors have made the claim indirectly.

4 'Demonstrate' means the authors have proven that the claim is true.

5 'Allege' means that the authors have made the claim but have not provided evidence.

Exercise 7

Model answer:

A number of theorists have attempted to explain human attraction. In a seminal study of student accommodation, Festinger, Schachter and Black (1950) concluded that proximity was a significant factor in determining who became friends with whom. Indeed the degree to which proximity seems to influence the forming of friendships appears, at first glance, to be remarkable. However, on more careful consideration, it is just as easy to conclude that what is being measured is not attraction so much as ease of opportunity. In other words, people make friends with those who are nearby not because they are attracted to them, but because they do not want to make the effort to look for friends further afield. Indeed, subsequent studies have challenged the Festinger *et al.* hypothesis. Newcomb (1963), for example, found that in the longer term, having similar attitudes overrode proximity as a factor in human attraction. Indeed, it is more likely that proximity, rather than being a factor in itself, could simply be an aspect of similarity. In other words, people may be attracted to those who live nearby because they are assumed to be similar.

Chapter 13

Exercise 1

1 The final four sentences of the introduction show that the student has correctly interpreted the essay question. The issue is discussed in relation to a particular country – Japan. The second and third sections cover the problem (= 'origins of the problem') and how it can be addressed (= 'recommendations').

2 Remove the sentences: 'The top computer manufacturers include IBM, Dell, Hewlett-Packard and Apple (HubPages, 2012). These companies are immensely profitable. Apple alone posted profits of £8.8 billion in the three months to July 2012. (Apple, 2012).' These sentences are not relevant to the discussion because they are about manufacturers of computer hardware not the internet.

Exercise 2

1 The reference list shows that writer has referred to a reasonable range of sources for an essay of this length. The entries are also correctly presented. However, some of the sources were published before 2009 and would normally be considered out-of-date for this type of topic. Use of the Young (1998) and Greenfield (1999) sources could be justified if the definitions they give are still widely used. The Ishii (2003) source, on the other hand, is too old to be used to illustrate the current situation.

In addition, two of the commercial sites used, HubPages and What Japan Thinks, would not be considered academically credible because the owners may have been paid to present the information in a certain way. The third site, Apple Press Info, although also commercial, would be acceptable because it is used as a primary source for information about company results.

2 In the two paragraphs, the writer uses two sources to define the term 'internet addiction' and two sources to support her claims about the nature of internet addiction in Japan.

3 The writer has done well to support her opinion with source material, but because she has not presented a range of different points of view, she has limited her scope for critical commentary. However, one of the strengths of the first

paragraph is that the writer does suggest that the definitions provided are not sufficiently specific to the Japanese context and therefore need to be further elaborated. This prepares the reader well for the following paragraphs where the writer explains what specific characteristics internet addiction takes in Japan.

4 Although possibly out-of-date, the sources are appropriately academic and fit the context of the student's essay. However, the first quote is longer than it needs to be for the purpose of this essay and the final quote is introduced without sufficient commentary. The student could have shown more skill in her use of sources by, for example:

a reducing the Young quote to: Young (1998: 237) defines internet addiction as 'an impulse-control disorder that does not involve an intoxicant.'

b using an author-prominent citation format to frame the final direct quote as an opinion and saying more about it, for example: 'In his thoughtful analysis of the predicament of internet users in Japan, Ito (2005: 16) argues "Although a limited form of contact, mobile e-mail has fulfilled a function akin to co-presence for people that lack the means to share the same private physical space."'

Exercise 3

In the first half of the paragraph, the writer makes an interesting point drawing together earlier ideas, that is, that the arrangement and use of space in Japanese internet cafes reflects they way Japanese young people have habitually used the internet. However, the second point regarding *hikikomori* is less well developed and not directly linked to previous ideas. The writer says the phenomenon is social in origin but does not fully explain or support the claim. She could for example, list the social factors that contribute to the emergence of *hikikomori* and explain how they interact.

Exercise 4

1 According to the writer's plan there are three main body sections: definitions of internet addiction, the problem in the Japanese context, and recommendations. There is also the

introductory paragraph itself as well as (possibly) a conclusion, making five sections in total.

2 The writer has written approximately 650 words, using 65% of the word limit.

3 The student has two further sections to write (approximately 40% of her material) and 35% of her word count left. She should therefore meet or slightly exceed her target.

Exercise 5

It is not easy to imagine completely eradicating internet addiction without eradicating the internet itself. ~~The internet has developed to the point where it is impossible to imagine life without it.~~ The internet is essential and part of daily life for many people. However, there may be ways of lessening the social isolation associated with excessive internet use if we look to what happens in countries outside of Japan. Many countries such as the UK, France, ~~Germany, France, Canada, the US,~~ and Australia, have widely available Local Area Network (LAN) hotspots where the public can have free ~~wireless~~ access to the internet through Wireless Fidelity (Wi-Fi). ~~Wi-Fi is a trademark of the Wi-Fi Alliance and it applies to devices that adhere to the Institute of Electrical and Electronics Engineers' standards number 802.11.~~ According to the Office for National Statistics (2009), 2.5 million people in the UK accessed the internet through Wi-Fi in 2009, compared to 700,000 people in 2007. Furthermore, not only public places such as airports or stations but also cafés and restaurants offer free wireless access to the internet. Japan, in contrast, has far less access to and knowledge of public Wi-Fi. In fact, in a recent study, 39.2 per cent of the internet users surveyed said that they were not familiar with public wireless LAN hotspots and 77.3 percent had never used a public wireless LAN from their laptop (What Japan Thinks, 2009). If wireless free LANs were more available in public places in Japan, people would be more likely to use the internet in public spaces rather than in private study rooms. People might use the internet more carefully because they can be observed publicly. Moreover, they would at least have the opportunity to combine face-to-face social interaction with online interaction, thereby reducing the isolation that is characteristic of internet addiction.

Exercise 6

Model answer:

Parents could also be made aware of the dangers of allowing their children unlimited access to the internet. The warning signs of internet addiction include: increasing use of the internet, irritability when denied access, deception regarding amount of internet use and repeated failure in attempts to stop or limit use (Young, 2012). These could be publicized so that parents can intervene early and explore the underlying reasons for the behaviour. Although early intervention alone is unlikely to solve the problem, it may reduce the likelihood of the problem becoming worse.

Exercise 7

To sum up, this essay has shown how has the internet influenced (**how the internet has influenced**) Japanese youth. Personalization of internet use, which began with the development of mobile phones, encouraged users to become increasing (**increasingly**) dependent on online communication. Today, the role of the internet in young people's lives has become more complex because it gives them something they need: a separate social space. The emergence of 'internet café refuges' and *hikikomori* indicate that internet addiction is also complex and connected to other social issues such as homelessness and poor mental health. Although it is impossible to know where internet technology will proceed in the future. Most (**future, most**) people would probably agree that they would not want to do without. Attempts to eradicate internet addiction are therefore likely to fail. However, there's (**there are**) possible avenues that can be explored. Making free wireless LANs more available could reduce the isolation associated with internet addiction. Secondly, making people more aware of the dangers of internet addiction could reduce it's (**its**) prevalence.

Exercise 8

The date is missing. The title could be put in a more formal font such as Times New Roman.

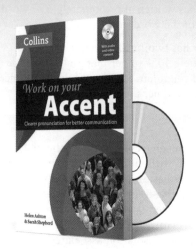